Waiting on the world

Waiting on the Word

*Preaching sermons that connect
people to God*

Lorraine Cavanagh

DARTON·LONGMAN+TODD

First published in 2017 by
Darton, Longman and Todd Ltd
1 Spencer Court
140 – 142 Wandsworth High Street
London SW18 4JJ

ISBN: 978-0-232-53262-3

A catalogue record for this book is available from the British Library

Phototypeset by Kerrypress, Markyate, St Albans.
Printed and bound by Bell & Bain, Glasgow.

For Connie, George, Emma and Lachlan

Contents

Foreword

Religion is that rich and interesting spiritual hinterland that lies in between God and humanity. It is the place of encounter and of reordering. That said, many of our assumptions about what constitutes a good Christian life are merely relative. But God is absolute. Which is why it takes a lifetime of discernment to understand and practice faith - only to find at the end of our lives, that we are mere beginners.

Such a lifetime can only ever be the most preliminary understanding of God. Wisdom is simply this: knowing your place before God. Wisdom is essentially about knowing that we really don't know very much; that God knows us in a way we can never know God. In God, our very depths are known.

Living the holy life is partly about separating ourselves from the world, and partly about engaging with it. It is partly about giving, and partly about receiving. It is partly about casting away, and partly about gathering. George Herbert (1593-1633), in a famous passage on sermons, tells us:

'... sermons are dangerous things ... [nobody] goes out of the church as he came in ... the parson procures attention, but the character of his sermon is holiness; he is not witty, or learned, or eloquent, but holy – by choosing texts of

devotion, not controversy, moving and ravishing texts …
and by dipping and seasoning all our words and sentences in
our hearts, before they come out of our mouths, and truly
affecting and cordially expressing all that we say…when thou
so teachest, we are all scholars …'. (Chapter 7, 'The Parson
Preaching', in *The Country Parson*)

It is in this vein that I warmly welcome and commend
Lorraine Cavanagh's excellent *Waiting on the Word*.

In some ways, sermons don't so much come to you, as the
very best catch you, unaware. They coax, tease and then draw
us in. They are honey traps. They are for falling in to. And
once ensnared, we realise that they are nectar. Towards the
end of the classic Pixar movie *Toy Story* (1995), Woody and
Buzz Lightyear find themselves in great peril as they attempt
to catch up with Andy's mother's car after the big removal
has happened. The packers have come, and everyone is
leaving home to start a new life in a new place.

Except that both Buzz and Woody are left behind, and
needing to catch up fast. Buzz is forced to fly … except that
it is not exactly flying – more of a big catapult, really. As
Woody says: 'That's not flying – that's just falling with style'.
It reminds me of Douglas Adams in *The Hitchhiker's Guide to
the Galaxy*: 'There is an art to flying. The knack lies in learning
how to throw yourself at the ground – and miss.'

When we speak of falling, we can barely conceive of it
in positive terms. To fall is dangerous: I have had a fall, and
broken a bone. Fallen leaders; fallen men or women. The Fall
is the end of the creation story in Genesis, and the beginning
of an epic salvation story. Jesus falls on the via dolorosa.
Jesus says 'unless a grain of wheat falls to the ground and

dies it cannot bear fruit'. He did not say 'unless a grain of wheat is planted'. He said 'fall'. Sermons fall on us; and we fall into their words.

Yet for many people, to fall is to fail. Cities fall; so do people. It is to be reduced: to come to nothing. And yet, we also fall in love. To fall is also to let go. It is also to go with the flow; to cascade, like a river or waterfall. Rainer Maria Rilke, in his *Book of Hours: Love Poems to God*, has this to say:

> How surely gravity's law,
> strong as an ocean current,
> takes hold of even the strongest thing
> and pulls it toward the heart of the world.
>
> Each thing -
> each stone, blossom, child -
> is held in place.
> Only we, in our arrogance,
> push out beyond what we belong to
> for some empty freedom.
>
> If we surrendered
> to earth's intelligence
> we could rise up rooted, like trees.
>
> Instead we entangle ourselves
> in knots of our own making
> and struggle, lonely and confused.
>
> So, like children, we begin again
> to learn from the things,

because they are in God's heart;
they have never left him.

This is what the things can teach us:
to fall,
patiently to trust our heaviness.
Even a bird has to do that
before he can fly.

Christianity is sometimes less about flying – and more about falling with style. Sermons are very much about falling in to God's arms, and less about struggling to soar upwards. As Dennis Potter noted, shortly before his own death: 'religion is not the bandage – it is the wound'. Good sermons mark us. They season us. They take us up to heaven. But they bring us back down to earth too. So we are asked not to fly from the pages we read or the words we hear, but first to fall – into God's arms. Good sermons receive us and welcome us, as God does.

Yet as Herbert says, a good sermon always changes us: nobody who hears one can ever be the same again. How important it is, then, that Lorraine has written this fine exploration of the need for the preacher to find space and peace to connect with God in order truly to connect with those who hear her talk. May the scriptural texts that ravish the hearer and feed our faith also transform the reader of this book, leading to deeper devotion and discipleship - and seasoning our spirituality.

The Very Revd Professor Martyn Percy
Dean of Christ Church, Oxford

Chapter 1

Preaching for a changing Church

The sermon is over. The relieved congregation gets to its feet for the Creed. No extraordinary encounter with God has taken place and many are already wondering what was said. They may even be wondering why they are there. And what of the preacher? Perhaps she is relieved too. She has got through another sermon. She is now wondering about the intercessions, and trying to remember what that notice was that she forgot to write down. She too is wondering why she is there. Meanwhile, the Creed goes on, more or less saying itself because the preacher, who is also leading the service, and who is not great at choral speaking, has momentarily lost track of where everyone has got to. As the Creed shuffles to a close, questions hang in the air, questions about the reality of God and the purpose of life.

Nobody is expecting much of an answer to these questions. None was forthcoming in the sermon. But the people had come to church, nevertheless, and they had waited, hoping to hear something which would connect with their need for God. The sermon had been largely anecdotal, dotted with 'asides' and personal stories. During the ensuing week, one or two of these personal anecdotes

1

and reminiscences surface in the minds of those who were sitting in the pews on Sunday, but they sense no connection with anything of profound or life-changing significance for them, no moment of truth, no deep and lasting epiphany with regard to their relationship with God.

They have good reason to wonder why they were there in the first place. But they were there all the same, and it is likely that they will return next week. They will return because it is their church, or because they like the vicar and want to support him,[1] or because their family is buried in its graveyard, or simply because the other people in the congregation are the only ones with whom they will exchange a few words, or experience ordinary human friendship during the coming week. If they are young, this may be a one-off visit. They may be looking to move on from their own church, a church which has only partially satisfied their need for God. They are surveying the field. These are the searchers after meaning and truth. They are changing churches for any one of a number of reasons, some related to style of worship or leadership but, more often, others pertaining to theological questions which they need to be helped to address, so that they can mature in their relationship with God.

The same goes for people who may be returning to church in early or later mid-life and whose needs are often overlooked when it comes to deciding on mission priorities, despite the fact that they often constitute a significant

---

1   I have used feminine and masculine gender pronouns, in a deliberately random way, throughout this book in order to emphasise the common nature of the preaching task, and of its challenges, and to avoid stereotypic representations of the preacher.

portion of the congregation.[2] They too are searching for truth and meaning. They need to feel valued and their gifts, as well as their intellectual and spiritual needs, taken seriously. They are often far more open to change than people assume. They may welcome a fresh approach to questions of doctrine and church polity. At the same time, they may want to re-connect with the faith they once had, and perhaps go back over their life history by placing it in a sacred context. But they will not necessarily want to find the church they once had, preserved as it always was, and peopled with a small ageing and dispirited band of die-hards who want to keep it that way.

Connecting

All of these people sense a need for silence, space and a sense of the sacred. They expect to find all three of these in their local church. They also sense that their local church, even if they seldom or never set foot in it, is a repository for a particular history, a story told through word and sacrament in such a way as to connect them personally with ultimate truth. Churches convey truth through being a particular kind of people. This is how they confirm the truth of the Christian story which they convey through the contextuality of their particular church. Their contextuality is the preaching, liturgy or worship of the Catholic and Protestant traditions. The

---

2   '25 years ago in the Church of England membership and attendance matched the national profile and population. Now attendees are 20% older than the National profile and 8 times more likely to attend at the age of 80 years than at 18 years.' Remarks taken from the minutes of the Monmouth Diocesan Conference, 17 October 2015.

story, which we call Salvation History, is essentially the same, but it is told with different emphases, according to contextuality.

The one who is immediately responsible for the telling of the story will be the preacher. He may not be a theologian, but he must have an innate sense of the meaning of this story and how it has impacted his own life. If preachers do not sense its truth in this way they will have nothing to say to their listeners. They must also bring to the task of preaching a particular sense of history, of the contextuality which has shaped their own life and that of their community. A sense of history and contextuality is vital to the maturing of the human person, not only in order to understand the workings of human nature and its implications for the politics and conflicts of the day, but to enable us to know who we are, how we can define ourselves in the borderless, limitless space created by a dominant a-historical materialist ethos. This is the challenge facing every preacher as well as the Church itself. Materialism, and its criteria for 'success', increasingly defines us, but it fragments the Body of Christ. As with the world, so with the Church. We are bombarded with mission incentives and action plans which equate with commercial propaganda designed to persuade us that we want and need a life-style (a successful church) which parodies what life in God is about. The more we buy into this, the more we want this artificial life, and the less true life we actually have. [3]

---

3   I am indebted to Maggie Ross for this line of thinking and for much that will follow from it in this book. See especially her *Silence: A User's Guide*, vol.1. (London: DLT, 2014), p. 225.

The Church, desperate to survive, has gradually become a hostage to fortune. Its survival priorities are such that it is now obliged to operate in the spiritual wasteland of secular materialism and to adopt its methods. These involve, among other things, managing buildings, devaluing its clergy and ignoring the gifts which many people, both ordained and lay, have to bring to its service, because their specific gifts do not fit with its own self-perception or with its short-term survival strategy. This often leads to institutional bullying which harms the Church and the people it exists to serve.[4]

I recently attended a deanery conference designed to promote the idea of ministry areas in our diocese, but like all strategic decisions reached in the wrong way, those selling it failed to enthuse their audience. In fact many of those present went away feeling angry, betrayed and disillusioned. Most were over 50 and at a rough estimate, probably around 65% of them were women. The meeting was orchestrated and driven by four men. Thanks to an articulate audience, it revealed quite clearly not only what is wrong with the institution, but what needs to happen to change it for the better. Changing the Church for the better is a matter of something happening to its people, rather than devising strategies which it is hoped will keep the organisation going.

Good strategy and planning exist to promote the life and happiness of an organisation, thereby making its work effective. But it is the Church's life in God, and its happiness in being God's people, which make it attractive to the world in the way Jesus was attractive. Jesus was attractive because

---

4   The following account is a précis of my blog post of 3 June 2015.

he gave people something which no organisation could take away from them, the knowledge that they mattered to God and permission to be happy in that knowledge. So life, which is knowing that we matter to God, and the happiness which that brings, preclude strategy. This deanery meeting suppressed both life and happiness. It was a dictatorial and thinly veiled underpinning of the same old order presented in the form of something new.

But people are not so easily fooled. The new system, as one person commented from the floor, would in fact ensure the continuing subsidisation of middle management and top ranking clergy, even though much lip service was paid to those training for lay ministry. There was also little acknowledgment of the faithfulness of unpaid priests whose services, I couldn't help feeling, are deemed by some to be less desirable than those of a stipendiary. Some people felt that too much was spent on buildings and that part of these expenses should be borne by other bodies. Many of these concerns were glossed over in a patronising way which only made for more hurt and anger.

The drive to survive

The Church is increasingly management led, because it is driven by the need to survive.[5] It has adopted the 'growth' mentality of a secular organisation but in doing so, it is rapidly losing sight of its true purpose, which is to be Christ

5   I am grateful to Martyn Percy for the substance of these reflections. See especially his 'Growth and Management in the Church of England: Some comments' in *Modern Believing: The Journal of Theological Liberalism*, vol.55, issue 3.

for the world of today, to be his compassion and his wisdom and to enact his justice in word and deed in all contexts and by all means available to it. In order to begin to do this, it needs to re-learn the kenotic self-forgetfulness which is a reflection of the self-emptying of Christ.[6] As it loses sight of its true purpose, it falls into a state of superficial semi-idolatrous self-contemplation. Its main priority becomes the maintaining of a public *figura*.[7] This is the outward image which it presents to the world and with which it is increasingly infatuated. It is manifested in a status-driven, hierarchical and still largely patriarchal system of governance with which many people feel increasingly at odds.

While this is a picture of the Church which many have grown to accept, it is a pale replica of what the Church could yet be. Its public *figura* obscures the greater and truer reality which is the heart of its life. What we see on the surface hides the reality of a God who yearns for his people and knows them intimately, and who also yearns for them to know him. Instead of sensing the mystery of God in a way which is unique to the act of worship, what people see on the surface of the Church's life, and therefore take the Church to be about, is 'busyness'. Instead of the reflection of the living and eternal God, they see a pale reflection of the transient busyness of the world, but without the sense of purpose and direction which keep secular organisations in touch with the needs of their market. The Church is busy with things

6   Maggie Ross, *Pillars of Flame: Power, Priesthood and Spiritual Maturity* (especially Chapter 5), (New York, Seabury Books, 2007).
7   The word *figura* is defined by *Collins Italian Dictionary* as having to do with appearance, or figure (as in cutting a foolish figure).

which do not seem to relate to the mystery of the on-going love of God for the world as it is, or with what those who are put off the Church really want. It is busy with its own politics, all of them returning, by one route or another, to the individual's longing for power and to the insecurity which feeds that longing.

To be in public ministry, whether ordained or lay, is to know power, and this is especially true for the one who is tasked with preaching.[8] There will come a point when the preacher will look up from her sermon notes, as she is preaching, and see the longing in the faces of the congregation. The people she is speaking to are waiting to meet God. At this precise moment the preacher will know what it means to 'hold' an audience. She will know power and she will know the meaning of true authority. She will also know that she is accountable to God for what she will say next and that she must not get in the way of the word which God wishes the people to hear. When this first happened to me, I realised that if I was to speak the words which God wanted his people to hear, I must discover the sermon's message anew for myself, as I was speaking it. For the preacher, the truth is conveyed in the moment it is discovered, so she must not get in the way of the work with her own 'agenda'. The preacher must be prepared to be surprised, to be taught, even as she is teaching.

---

8   God bestows power and authority without partiality on both women and men when they preach. This is what the religious establishment fears most about women as preachers. 'The authority of testimony is so powerful – more powerful ... than any authority conferred by a governing body', Anna Carter Florence, *Preaching as Testimony* (London: John Knox Press, 2007), p.67.

She must also be confident. Preaching is about confident performance.[9] Good preaching uses theatrical language in order to 'suspend disbelief', itself a theatrical term originally coined by S.T. Coleridge. For the preacher this means creating a conceptual space in the minds and hearts of those listening in which they receive, and are nourished by, the word of God. To suspend disbelief is to engage people's imagination and so make it possible for them to step outside the familiar and perceive new realities, a new truth, in a familiar text. The difference between truth and myth is not whether a statement is true in a propositional sense, but whether it resonates with love and, in the context of preaching, whether it re-awakens love for God.

The one preaching will have connected with God's people at a deep personal level. But she will also be holding to the same thread which connects her with God 'at all times and in all places', to quote from one of the Eucharistic prayers. Because of this two-way connection, what she says will resonate with something which her listeners may have always known, but now understand in a new way, in this moment of connection. It will be a kind of 'epiphany'.[10] The way the preacher speaks from her own place of vulnerability to God will draw people to her, and this makes her powerful. But the power is not hers to hold on to. She must allow it to return back to God through that same line of connectivity.

Those who are either coming to church for the first time, or returning after a prolonged absence, possibly because of

---

9   See Chapter 8.
10   James Joyce, *Stephen Hero*, John J. Slocum and Herbert Cahoon (eds.) (New Directions edition, 1963), p. 213.

a life crisis or bereavement, will be looking to connect with the kind of truth which gives coherence to their lives at this particular time. In other words, they will be in search of meaning. They will expect to find it in the context of both word and sacrament.[11] They may have occasionally sensed it in other contexts; through music, a good novel, or a poem. Or they may have known it as an instant of illumination, of sudden deep understanding, coming as a chance remark from friend or stranger. These moments of truth embed themselves in a person's memory. They are held in the subconscious, often for years. It is the task of the preacher to allow God to give coherence to these memories. One could argue that the suspension of disbelief is therefore the sermon's true purpose and that the sermon has served its purpose when it has effected a kind of self-emptying in the congregation, making space for a deeper perception and understanding of the text of the day and of the events and wider social context which shaped it. The good news of the Gospel emerges from within a kenotic self-emptying which allows us to see things as they really are, through the eyes of Christ.

The listener, as well as the preacher, must hear this good news as if for the first time, so that it cannot be something which the preacher generates with his own limited intellect, or solely from within his own experience. Both these approaches risk distorting the meaning of a text even as the preacher is trying to make immediate connections with what he imagines are the experiences of his listeners. He must

---

11   James A. Wallace, *Preaching to the Hungers of the Heart: The Homily on the Feasts and within the Rites,* Chapter3, (Collegeville: Liturgical Press, 2002).

have a sense of contextuality, of all the circumstances that shape a person's life, but he must also stand outside.[12] He must retain his objectivity so that he can be ready to respond in the moment to the people's hunger for God.

People coming to church for the first time, or returning to it after a prolonged absence, may feel a certain 'pull'; a sense that what the Church and the Christian faith have to offer will satisfy their perhaps unacknowledged hunger for God. The preacher's task is to bring them to a realisation that this hunger can be satisfied. She will do this through a balanced and nuanced presentation of the good news, which connects with the hearts and minds of her listeners. She must therefore create a state of equilibrium between affect and reason.[13] She must also resist the temptation to lure them back next Sunday, which would give them the impression that God refuses to meet them outside a 'same time, same place' routine. They must leave the church knowing that God wants them for himself and is already meeting them wherever they are, but that there is also a place for them in this particular 'mansion'.

Jesus promised that there would be many mansions in his Father's house (John 14:2). Some, but not all, will be found in the Church as we know it. Each person's journey is their own. They may travel by different paths but their ultimate destination, a place of communion in God, is the same. It is the task of the preacher to help them along the way. The

---

12   Lesslie Newbigin, *The Gospel in a Pluralist Society*, Chapter 12, 'Contextualisation: True and False', (London: SPCK 1989).
13   Kate Bruce, *Igniting the Heart: Preaching and Imagination* (London: SCM, 2015), p.15. See also Ian McGilchrist, 'Primacy of Affect' in *The Master and His Emissary* (Yale University Press, 2012), p.184.

preacher will be helping them to make sense of the promises of Scripture by suggestion rather than instruction. He will sense their real underlying questions, as the apostle Philip did when he responded to the official's invitation to explain a text from the prophecy of Isaiah. Philip listened to the man's questions, addressing them in the way given to him by God for that particular moment and set of circumstances. The official then asked to be baptised in a conveniently nearby river before going on his way. This is a fairly good approximation of what people returning to church might experience when they hear a good sermon.[14]

Something comparable happened to the congregation who heard Jesus as he preached on the mountainside about what makes for true happiness. He told them things they had always known in their hearts but which had been forbidden to them in the context of formal religious teaching, so their hearts, as well as their minds, needed to be set free. As a preacher he did not simply break with convention. He was a liberator.

In his sermon on the mount, Jesus tells the people that those who know they need God are free. The key to real freedom lies in admitting our need for God. He tells them that those who grieve, or whose grief is manifested as anger in the face of injustice, oppression and the corruption of power, will not have grieved in vain. Their grief and their anger are shared by God who has taken these passions into himself. He told them to wait on the unfailing love of God who is their ultimate vindicator.

---

14   Especially if there is coffee after the service, allowing opportunity for further discussion with those present as well as with the preacher.

Waiting

Waiting is central to the teaching of Jesus. It is only in waiting that we become good teachers ourselves. Jesus waited out his first thirty years in obscurity. He then waited in the wilderness for forty days, a day for each of the years spent by the Jews in the wilderness with God's presence about them as fire and cloud. And he waits for the Church to be renewed in its prophetic witness to the world of today. He waits for it to emerge from a spiritual wilderness of its own making, one in which it no longer hears the silent Word because of the ambient noise it creates in the busyness of its life. In such a climate of anxious self-preoccupation, including current obsessions about sexual mores, the Church cannot connect with the secret truth of God which people long to hear for themselves. Simone Weil, a Jewish philosopher who fled Europe in the early years of World War II, and whose book *Waiting on God* describes the intellectual struggle which led to her ultimate baptism, writes: 'The word of God is the secret word. He who has not heard this word, even if he adheres to all the dogmas taught by the Church, has no contact with truth.'[15]

This is how the institutional Church is perceived by many people who have long since stopped going to church on a Sunday. Their local church has become a space which, though beautiful, does not connect them with God or help them to connect him with the hopes and longings which shape their lives. They may still see it as a spiritual resource

---

15 Simone Weil, *Waiting on God*, Emma Craufurd (tr.), (Glasgow: Collins Fount, 1951).

but they cannot identify with it. It does not speak to them, so they do not want to belong.[16] But this reality is hard to quantify in managerial terms. Where there is no deep life of the spirit, the church's success or failure is measured according to the materialist criteria of the world. Churches must be seen to justify their existence, and clergy theirs, by filling pews. Where the success ethic informs a church's life the congregation becomes a commodity and, if it is a large one, something of a status gauge for the cleric. The cleric (if still relatively young) who is on his way up the Church career ladder will seldom stay for long in a struggling group of country parishes. When he moves on, the people are left feeling that they are ultimately of little real significance. They are part of someone else's career plan and they feel they have failed, because they are small and insignificant compared to many more successful churches, including, perhaps, the one to which their priest is moving. They feel unloved and let down by the Church.

Anxiety

Our anxiety about numbers is a reflection of the growth mentality which drives modern politics and economics. It also translates directly into the way we go about worship and preach sermons. Here, I am not referring to method. That will come later. I am talking about the kind of anxiety which deadens a church's life and casts a pall of self-doubt over those called to minister, whether lay or ordained. We

---

16   Alan Billings, *Secular Lives, Sacred Hearts: The Role of the Church in a Time of No Religion* (London: SPCK, 2004), p.12.

worry about getting *through* things, be it liturgy or preaching, and we worry about getting everything right, so that more people come to church next week. But does worrying about what we are to say or do allow us to connect with people on a Sunday morning? Do our anxious faces and words touch them where they hurt most? This is especially important in times of individual or collective trauma. Do we believe what we are saying? Does what we say connect us and our listeners more deeply to each other as the Body of Christ?

The answers to these questions do not lie solely in technique or intellectual ability. On the contrary; they are found in the extent to which we, as preachers, are prepared to be vulnerable, to know ourselves as very fragile vessels. Some of the best sermons I have heard have come from people who struggle with speech, have difficulty making clear connections, or simply don't look the part. Truth, the good news of the Gospel, seems to break through in their pauses and stumbling with words, often more vividly and with greater immediacy than it might in a sermon which has been honed to perfection and delivered with wit and *panache*. It seems that St Paul himself belonged to this category of preachers, but he knew how to speak to whatever situation his listeners were experiencing.

As I write this, we are witnessing the horrors of the Paris massacre of 13 November 2015. More than a hundred people have been slaughtered in cold blood in a homicidal lust for power worked out in the perversion of a good religion. Like others, this violent incident shows us that darkness that calls itself light is the deception which spawns the purest evil. The response to this brutally manifested lie has been an outpouring of prayer and of messages of solidarity with the French people and with the families of the victims. The anguish and the anger have also been expressed through silence. People are drawing together in the streets of Paris, standing in solidarity and prayer. Some may visit their local church this Sunday, perhaps after a long absence. Others are already doing so, lighting candles or simply sitting in the cool silence, trying to make sense of the chaos, trying to sense God's touch, to know that he grieves with them.

If they come on Sunday, they will be hoping to experience something of the answering grief of God in the face of such violence, although they may not define it in specific terms, except in the wordless desire which is lodged in the essence of their being, both individually and collectively. They will want to know that he is in solidarity with them, that their prayer is met by his mighty compassion. They will be looking for some kind of encounter with the holy in the face of such evil. They will also want to sense around them the 'communion of saints', those people gifted with the compassion of God who know when to speak and when not to. If they come on Sunday they will hope to hear something of this compassion in the words spoken to them by whoever is preaching. But they will not want to be evangelised.

Mission and evangelism are two words which have been conflated in such a way that their separate meanings have been obscured by the anxiety which they both convey. Mission, with its emphasis on service, has been compromised by the marginalisation of the very people whom Jesus would be most likely to befriend. It has also come to signify a climate of general activism which exhausts all those involved, leaving them little in the way of emotional resources with which to wait on people who simply need to be heard. Similarly, the good news embodied in the word 'evangelism' is often not very good for the marginalised. It can sound patronising when all they want is to be accepted unconditionally, to be understood and loved. Jesus did his evangelism through identifying with those who were at odds with the system and very much on the edge of society. He was not even part of the formal religious establishment, since he did not descend from the tribe of Levi, but from that of Judah. He was a 'borderland' person.[17] He encountered people who, for socio-historical reasons, were on the margins of society. This is where the Church of today needs to be if the people it is striving to reach through mission and evangelism are to encounter him in their times of need.

It follows that the most effective preachers will be those who can meet people in this borderland place. Their speaking will be authentic because they themselves will have experienced marginalisation in some way, either in the context of the Church, or in the wider context of their own life experience. A person who has not known what it is to be marginalised, to not quite fit in with whatever context they happen to be in, or who has never known loss or rejection, cannot preach in a way which connects deeply with anyone listening to them. In fact, they will not connect with *anyone* if they have not been tested in this way.

The time Jesus spent in the wilderness before he began his preaching ministry was a time of testing. He learned to know himself, as we all must know ourselves, and he had to experience the seduction of power. He was tempted to

---

17   L. William Countryman, *Living on the Border of the Holy: Renewing the Priesthood of All* (Harrisburg: Morehouse Publishing, 1999), p. 47.

believe that he could achieve results without facing the desire for power and instant gratification with which we all have to come to terms before we can become effective preachers. The preacher must go through the same testing process. She must know herself before God if she is to find not simply words, but an intelligent and wise heart of her own with which to meet people where they are, in all their longings and fears, on a Sunday morning.

Chapter 2

What is a sermon?
The search for meaning

Webster's dictionary defines preaching as 'to give moral or religious advice, especially in a tiresome manner'. The sermon has a bad track record. Many people associate preaching with Victorian piety, or with a particular theology or churchmanship, or with charismatic individuals whose showmanship they distrust. In all of these real or imagined settings the sermon is perceived as alienating. People feel that they have been manipulated or brainwashed, if not plainly bored.

Whether they come to church in an enquiring frame of mind, or just feel the need for God, churchgoers do not always look forward to the sermon. It is something which they will have to endure, or which may simply afford some time for doing a little mental darning, going over the past week, picking up stray threads and weaving them back into the garment of their life and relationships, filling the gaps so as to make better sense of things. The sermon does not help them make sense of their lives. At best, it is a series of answers to irrelevant questions. But the listener is hopeful. He waits to hear something that will resonate with his intuition, that will strike a note of truth, even if he knows that this is unlikely to happen. Others will have known in the first minute or two that the sermon was not going to have anything to say to them. It was something that the preacher had written out and then 'delivered' either as a formulaic working through of a given text or as a personal and predictable response to specific events. Somewhere during the course of its preparation the sermon had become an object, a stone which sinks to the bottom of the lake when it should have spun and hopped a few times first. It had been reduced to a matter of 'throwing answers like stones at the heads of those who have not yet asked the questions'.[1] The stones had disappeared from sight before they, or any questions they might have prompted, had the slightest chance of sinking into the inner consciousness of those listening.

Jesus did not preach sermons. He talked to people, so they went away more aware of who they were, of how they belonged in the deepest sense to God. They went away fed, sometimes bodily as well as intellectually and emotionally. At times, he shocked or angered them, although he did not always intend to do so or, if he did, it was only to give them a glimpse of what they were missing. He wanted them to know what it feels like to be fully alive, what we experience when we are fully engaged with another person or with an idea.

His first recorded sermon took place in his local place of worship on an ordinary Sabbath morning. He was handed

---

1   Paul Tillich, *Systematic Theology* (Chicago: University of Chicago Press, 1951).

the scroll with the text for the day which was a compilation of verses from the prophet Isaiah (Isaiah 61:1-2; 58:6) with added references to Leviticus. He did not address the congregation from an elevated podium or pulpit. He sat down, as was the custom for preachers.

Pulpits have their advantages; it is easier for the preacher to be seen, and perhaps heard, but pulpits also create a physical separation between the one speaking and those who are listening. This reinforces a further separation created by a top-down hierarchical system of governance in the institutional Church. People are feeling increasingly out of touch with the higher ranking clergy, and patronised by them, especially where the roles of administration and management are conflated with those of pastoral and spiritual care. The existing preaching environment in most churches mirrors this separation and can alienate those who are in the pews. They see the person who is preaching as a member of the *cognoscenti* standing over them, delivering a sermon from on high.

Speaking from 'on high' also gives the impression that a further separation exists between life as it is lived in the everyday, and life as it is intended to be lived in God. The people represent 'the everyday', and the preacher, talking down to them from the pulpit, seems to belong to another more rarefied sphere, so creating the impression that he or she has a 'hot line' to God and speaks on God's behalf. The Holy Spirit, whose living presence should fill the speaker and her listeners in equal measure, bears no relation to a 'hot line' to God. The alienation created by this more implicit separation is one of the aspects of preaching which puts many people off sermons, and puts them off coming to church.

How much better it would be if the preacher was to be seated, perhaps on a slightly raised surface, if visibility is a problem, with the people around her.[2] Being on the same level, and in much closer proximity to our listeners, makes it easier for us to sense whether what we are saying engages them, whether it is the truth they need to hear. A warm and reasonably comfortable environment is also helpful, as I have often found on visiting churches in the US. Warm churches make for greater attentiveness and for prayerful listening. They warm the mind. A congenial environment relaxes people and disposes the listener, as well as the person preaching, to expect the best from the sermon and to listen deeply for the truth they all need to hear. Only when people sense this shared truth will the sermon convey meaning.

Meaning

Meaning, or truth, comes in the epiphany moments which we all experience from time to time as moments of truth. But it also comes with deep listening and from living in such a way as to be available to God who is truth itself, in all our waking moments, as well as in our sleeping ones. Simone Weil describes this availability to God as *disponibilité*,

---

2   This works both in a formal liturgical setting and in smaller informal contexts, such as house communions or agapés. The St Gregory of Nyssa Episcopal Church in San Francisco not only has the preacher seated but invites the whole congregation to follow her from the preaching space to the altar when the creed has been said. This transitional movement, from word to sacrament, creates a people-based connection to the Eucharist and ties the sermon more closely to the rest of the service.

a permanent openness to God and to the unexpected.[3] It is also what Paul meant when he urged his readers to pray at all times. The one who is preaching needs to be open to being surprised by God at all times. If he is to convince others of the truth of what he is saying he must live from within that truth. If he is living within it he will have recognised that the faith which he professes through his sermon does not entirely depend on the literal or historical accuracy of facts and events. It depends on the truthfulness of his own dialogue with God. He is not putting forward an argument to prove or disprove facts. He is 'exposing' (from which we get the words 'expository preaching') the deeper meaning of Scripture for the present set of circumstances. He is taking his listeners beyond the rational, while using the rational as a springboard from which to expose a deeper truth. In order to arrive at the kind of truth which reaches beyond the rational, he will have thought honestly about it, respectful of the different ways in which a text can be read and of the intellectual and spiritual challenges which they present to him personally. He will have done his theology.

The sermon is an exhortation to the listener to take theology seriously. Theology is heart thinking. To think about God, or to do theology, is to be willing to be *disponible*, open to the risks entailed in working at a loving relationship so that it can mature and remain charged with meaning. The sermon should be an invitation to the listener to step outside the boundaries of the philosophy of religion, to be willing to change. It should invite her to explore beyond the purely

3   Simone Weil, *Cahiers*.

rational, beyond the mind which questions the 'existence' of God, a question which is often defeated by the very notion of existence as it might pertain to God. Among other things, the sermon should embody the possibility of open but honest trust with regard to the kind of God revealed through Scripture, and whether God is 'good' in the way we understand that word.

All of these questions provide a framework in which the truth about God in relation to human beings is worked out through Christian doctrine. But doctrine itself must be kept alive and constantly renewed by the collective mind of the Church as the whole people of God. It must come alive in the new truths which will emerge from the preacher's sermon on any Sunday morning in the context of their immediate needs. The congregation is not to be thought of as a non-specific collective. The congregation is not an 'it'. The congregation is a 'they'. They are God's people, unique persons who are gathered together to hear what God's Spirit has to say to them as a community and as persons honoured and loved by God.

When the preacher makes it possible for people to know themselves as loved by God, both together and individually, they become a worshipping community in the fullest sense. Luke describes Jesus offering this subtle transformation to the people in his local synagogue, an offer which they ultimately rejected. (Luke 4:16-22) The substance of his address would have unsettled some of them because it spoke directly into their collective situation; they were living under foreign occupation and they were not theologically free. They were controlled both by a foreign government and by the religious establishment. They were accustomed to hearing sermons which controlled how they thought and which would have made them feel intellectually safe. But sermons preached in a controlling mind-set, whether by leaders of sects within the Church, or by the religious establishment as a whole, do not convey love, so they do not convey meaning. Jesus spoke to the people, and to each person, in the heart's secret place, that place known only to God, where a person's fears and longings, as well as loves and hatreds, are lodged. He spoke freedom into the secret fears of many of his listeners. Those of us who preach are called to do the same.

In his first documented preaching engagement, the text appointed for the day suited his purpose admirably. It was about the Jubilee year which occurred once every fifty years, to coincide with the Day of Atonement (Lev. 25:8-13). The Jubilee was ordained as a time of returning. The Jews were to return to their place of birth and re-gather as tribes and families. It was also to be a time of rest for the land and of freedom for those in bonded labour. In the final words of his address Jesus reveals to the people that he embodies the truth of this prophecy 'Today this Scripture has been fulfilled in your hearing'. He reveals a truth which they recognise as an epiphany, something which they have perhaps known for a long time but have not wished to come to terms with. Some marvel at his wisdom. Others are outraged because he has overstepped the lines of convention when it comes to who has the right to speak the truth in the context of gatherings that support the edifice of institutionalised religion.

As preachers, we are called to speak the truth as Jesus spoke it to that congregation, whatever the text of the day, and however formal the setting. We are called to embody the liberating truth given to us in the abiding Spirit of Christ and to manifest that truth in our own life in God. When the sermon speaks truth from within the preacher's life in God, as it did when Jesus addressed the people of Nazareth, the preacher will immediately connect with people wherever they are in their own unique relationship with him. She will connect at the level of intuitive knowing, or what the Anglican solitary, Maggie Ross, calls 'deep mind'.[4]

Our inner, or deeper life in God, has its own dynamic. It is always about 'returning'. Our life in God is our place of Jubilee. The prophet Isaiah speaks into the confusion and doubt of people who are being urged to return from a place of exile (540BC). They have settled into leading quite comfortable if somewhat colourless lives, but he urges them not to be afraid to return, but to believe in this deep inner place, which is their collective deep mind and where their real identity as a people lies. 'In returning and rest you shall be saved' (Isaiah 30:15) the prophet writes.[5] He is calling them into truth, as a people who are forgiven and reconciled to God. He urges them to trust that God will provide for them as his people, and to trust in the deeper truth which they share. If they grasp this offer, the peace it gives will transform them into people who are fully alive, the kind of people they were chosen to be when he first called their father Abraham out of the land of Ur.

The truth about the Christian idea of salvation consists in a similar new beginning, in returning to God who makes a new creation of our lives, past and present. It is a return

---

4   Ross, *Silence*, pp.41ff and p.76.

5   Their national, as well as their spiritual identity is brought together in this verse which scholars have argued is the pivotal point of the whole of the book of Isaiah.

to a truth already known, the reality of God's love for the human race. The sermon will always return to this central aspect of Christian doctrine, not necessarily by stating it in so many words, but by inference. The preacher will infer its truth by being a certain kind of person, a bearer of the sacramental and transformative word of God.[6] So the preacher must have great love for God if he is to be an agent of transformation and if his sermon is to be sacramental in the fullest sense. A sacramental sermon is one which feeds its listeners. It is the prelude to the Eucharistic meal, the 'starter'. Archbishop Donald Coggan compares the sermon to the act of consecration itself, so that in preaching 'The "elements" are words, ordinary words, the words that we constantly use in the commerce of everyday life …Who can doubt', he asks 'that, when such preaching takes place, there is the Real Presence of Christ?'[7]

Being a transformative agent is not a matter of having a forceful personality. Preachers who rely on their personality to win over their congregation risk obscuring the delicate truth which is at the heart of the message. They obscure the word with their personality and in doing so they are treating their congregation as an 'it' and not as a 'they'. The truth which they obscure also needs to be liberated from the kind of constraints imposed by *a priori* suppositions about text and theology. In extreme cases, these *a priori* judgments can cause serious psychological harm to God's people, especially

6   Kay L. Northcutt, *Kindling Desire for God: Preaching as Spiritual Direction*, (Minneapolis: Fortress Press, 2009), p.29.
7   Donald Coggan, *Preaching: The Sacrament of the Word* (New York: The Crossroad Publishing Company, 1988), p.76.

to women and to those who are marginalised or excluded from churches on the basis of their sexual orientation.

The truth, as it always returns both the preacher and the listener to the love of God, is the meaning and purpose of any sermon, but it will be given and received in a myriad of ways, depending on a person's particular circumstances and on the way their thinking about meaning and the world has already been shaped by their own life experience. This applies in equal measure to both preacher and listener. Relying on personality alone will obscure the message sooner or later, when the charisma starts to wear thin and reveals little intellectual or spiritual substance beneath it. To cultivate a personality in order to win over those we are speaking to, in order to make them like us, is to deal in untruthfulness. A truthful person is always transparent in the way she relates to others and in her relationship with God. She is not constrained by the Church she serves and she does not hide behind its ramparts. She does not allow it to obscure her humanity. She is someone people would warm to in any other context. This is the kind of person Jesus was.

Jesus was fully human, earthed in the fullest sense, as holy people invariably are. Holiness is not a matter of introspective detachment from life, or from other people. It is about being fully *in* the world, with all its confusion and its physical and emotional needs, but not *of* the world. The preacher who connects with her listeners is someone who they recognise, as if they had always known her, because she speaks from a place they know. She is *in* the world. She is not trying to conform to the expectations of the world, or to the worldly expectations of the institutional Church, although she is the Church's public face. Here she has a choice; she can be one of two different faces, depending on the depth and veracity of her life in Christ. She can be the *figura* of the institutional Church, or the face of Christ to his people. If she is to be the face of Christ to them, people will need to feel that they matter to her and that her love for them is not compromised by concerns over protecting her territory or by 'profile' grabbing. Her true self, or 'self-consciousness', and the things that matter to her, will be shaped by her inner life in Christ.[8] This is the basis of holiness, both for the Church and for the person who serves it, or who speaks on its behalf.

Holiness has nothing to do with achievement or success, especially in regard to ministry. Once understood, this takes considerable pressure off clergy, since letting go of the drive to achieve and succeed immediately places us outside the system. The same applies to the way we preach. A good sermon does not simply impress. Impressive sermons are often quickly forgotten, either because they leave people feeling intellectually inadequate, or because they are devoid of the kind of substance which nourishes the heart as well as the mind. They are no longer subject to the Holy Spirit; the impressive sermon has become 'my sermon', which I will store on my computer and use again. This is to systematize and objectify the word of God. Where it should have been inherently fluid and supple, able to shape itself to the moment and to the hearts of the listeners, the sermon now belongs to the preacher. It has become something which the preacher owns and arbitrarily 'drops' on the heads of the people. It has become a commodity, wholly unrelated to

8   Maggie Ross describes this as the 'en-Christing process', *Writing the Icon of the Heart*, p.46.

their deeper fears and longings and which they will probably have heard before, in any case.

Objectified sermons are the shadow-side of a Church which is becoming systematized. They are its *figura*. Systems survive by telling those who serve them that they must meet certain expectations and that they should achieve numerical growth, generally described as 'mission'. For the Church, part of the achievement process consists in justifying its existence on the secular high street by offering the right commodities, commodities which replicate perceived social trends but which often lack depth and meaning. Systems, and the commodities which serve them, disconnect us from God, from people and from our own humanity. [9]

When Jesus tells his disciples not to be afraid because his kingdom is 'not of the world', he meant that neither he nor his kingdom are of the system. He is telling us the same thing today. We are not to fear the system, because we have already been freed from it. Wherever the Church has allowed itself to become over systematized, the abiding Spirit of Jesus remains a threat, because his Spirit is about freedom, a freedom which he continues to offer to those who preach in his name.

When Jesus tells his disciples to go out and make disciples, he is telling them to be liberators, to set the captives free. The first few seconds of any sermon are decisive in this respect. Is the sermon going to bring hope to the captive? Does it invite her to return to a God in whom she will find peace?

---

9   My thinking owes much to Maggie Ross's depiction of the Church as organization. See *Pillars of Flame: Power, Priesthood and Spiritual Maturity* (New York: Church Publishing, 2007), Chapter 6.

If the preacher has connected with them at any point in the sermon, individuals will approach him after the service and remark on the fact that his words touched them, or that he sparked off a new way of thinking about a text. Both of these areas of transformation will generate a 'ripple', or 'trickle down' effect. Both will be transformative. The way the words connect or kindle something in the heart of the listener will perhaps manifest itself in some kinder attitude or action to another person later in the week, someone who may never come near a church. This is mission at its best. It proceeds from a silence in which we, as preachers, are called to abide and wait if we are to kindle any semblance of faith in the hearts of those who listen to us.

How we think about a given text is a germinating process which happens in our inner silence, but its truth is rarely given before the moment of speaking. It will be conveyed not only through words but through the whole of the person who is doing the speaking, effecting deep transformative changes on that person, and on those listening. A sermon must have its own particular truth. Its truth will free both listener and preacher from habits of mind which may have become a constraint to them spiritually and so impeded their growth into theological maturity. The newness of the thought, and the liberation which that brings, comes in the moment. The thought has not been 'kept in reserve', or re-cycled from a previous sermon. It pertains to the moment and to the on-going life of the Holy Spirit. The more such ideas are allowed to surface from the preacher's inner silence, the greater the liberating potential of the sermon.

The sermon, if it is truly liberating, frees both speaker and listener in a downward direction, from the mind to the heart.

It takes us into the realm of intuition. Here, the mind and the unconscious function together, so that we learn from what is said through us as we preach. We think and sense at the same time. In neurological terms, this might correspond to the intuitive process described by clinical psychologist, Daniel Siegel, an 'input from the body [which] forms a vital source of intuition and powerfully influences our reasoning and the way we create meaning in our lives.'[10] We input with our rational minds and subject the rational process to our love for God. The sermon's liberating power consists in freeing all of us for the faith journey which lies ahead, the journey towards God which preacher and people take together. Thus, the sermon will be the preacher's *locus* of encounter with God, and God's *locus* of encounter with his people.

Journeying

Journeying has shaped the Judeo-Christian tradition from Abraham to Moses and the later exilic prophets, to the peripatetic teaching ministry of Jesus. The idea of journey, or pilgrimage, continues to shape the life of the Church today. It is a context in which we meet God. People grow in their relationship with God, and they grow as a worshipping community, in the context of movement, migration and change, and through waiting. The journeying is in the waiting. In Old Testament times, God's people waited to encounter him in the 'tent of meeting' at Sinai. They wept and waited

10   In James D. Whitehead and Evelyn Eaton Whitehead, *Nourishing the Spirit: The Healing Emotions of Wonder, Joy, Compassion, and Hope*, 'How we know – Intuition and the Wisdom of the Body' (Maryknoll, NY: Orbis Books, 2012), p.150.

by the waters of Babylon. Later, they waited for Jesus to heal a child or a loved servant, or to raise a brother from the tomb. Today, the Church waits for the renewal of its life in God. The waiting is part of the journey.

Biblical journeys often took decades. They symbolise the faith journey which we are all called to undertake from the first moment of consciousness, the moment when we discern a face and know that a vital bond exists between us and that person, until our last breath. A person's faith journey passes through various stages. In his study on faith development, James Fowler compares these stages to the life transitions which occur from early infancy to adult maturity.[11] While his theory is helpful in providing a framework within which to explain the way we mature in our thinking about God and the development of moral awareness, it remains within the bounds of the explainable.

The preacher must be prepared to take us outside the explainable, outside defining frameworks. She must journey with people who are looking for a way out of the confines of institutionalised religion, and through the spiritual wilderness of materialist individualism, into fellowship with God and into a renewed understanding of what it means to be God's people. She must journey with them, but at the same time wait with them, so that she can meet them in this undefined wilderness place. In order to do this, and prior to speaking to them, she will have already engaged in a kind of silent exploration of the wilderness as her listeners might be

11   James Fowler, 'Stages of Faith Development' in Philip Richter and Leslie J. Francis, *Gone But Not Forgotten: Church Leaving and Returning* (London: DLT, 1998), Chapter 5.

experiencing it, visualising their faces, if she knows them, or their presence with her if she does not. She will have waited on the word which God wishes to speak to them. Identifying with them in this way in the preceding days will give meaning to the words she speaks on the Sunday. As she begins to speak to them she will sense that she knows them, even if she has never met them, that she has travelled alongside them in a kind of dynamic stillness, always travelling and at the same time always arriving at a place already known.

Perhaps Lewis Carroll was thinking of this when he imagined The Red Queen running with Alice.[12] They were running so fast that things seemed to be running with them, but at the same time nothing ever changed, everything remained still. This particular incident in Carroll's story is a metaphorical rendering of the dynamic of stillness. The preacher must allow her thoughts to come from within the still dynamic of her own deep mind which is the only place from which she will connect with the intuitions and feelings of the people and with the deep mind of the individual. She must run with them, so that they can be still in God, so that they can 'return' to him. She must journey with them in a spirit of forgiveness, speaking to a people who have been forgiven in Christ. For this to be possible, she must journey from within her own life narrative, but without distracting their attention from Christ by drawing attention to herself.[13]

The preacher undertakes the journey with the people, as the prophets did, but he is also called to teach and guide

---

12   Lewis Carroll, *Alice Through the Looking Glass*, Chapter 2.
13   Brian Castle, *Reconciliation: The Journey of a Lifetime* (London: SPCK, 2014), p.74.

along the way. His words must be food for the journey. So the one who is tasked with preaching sermons should expect to do so from his own wilderness place. Only then will he connect with the deep longings and the anguish secretly held in the hearts of others. His own anguish will be the on-going inner conflict which is part of every journey undertaken in a primal desire to be at one with the purposes of God, even if that desire is unrecognised or consciously resisted.

As we meander through the wilderness of life, a wilderness which we sometimes either choose or create for ourselves, we sooner or later realise that the purposes of God are for our true well-being, found only in him. This does not mean that the sermon should meander, as sermons do when they try to be simply 'relevant'. The sermon should lead preacher and people together along the straight path chosen by Christ, embracing them while pressing forward, attuned to the same Spirit which journeyed in the wilderness of the biblical exile, behind and ahead of his people until they reached the promised land.

It follows that a good sermon will re-awaken a person's longing for God by bringing them to a new place, a place of meeting. A good sermon will open up a new theological landscape. It will 'transfigure' the way they see things. It will allow for metaphor.[14] Every event in Scripture, irrespective of historical detail, is also a metaphor, so everything we say as preachers has a deeper *metaphorical* dimension which will touch people in the way a straightforward account will not.

---

14   Maggie Ross differentiates between the idea of something which is transfigured, and that of transformation, the latter being a word which is often misunderstood and therefore misused.

Like the story of the Transfiguration of Christ on the holy mountain, miracles and many of the events we speak about can also be read as 'a narrative about changed perspective'.[15] Changed perspective changes, or deepens, our understanding of the world as it is, and of how the world's suffering connects with the anguish and longings of those to whom we preach sermons. It relates their longing for God to their longing for truth and righteousness, and it assures them of its value to God. It prepares the way for empathy, for transfigured understanding leading to change.

Empathy is the basis for real missional action. The Church of the future will have been rooted in empathy, in a capacity for understanding and in the healing which comes with it. In the next chapter I shall be looking at how the encounter with God, effected between preacher and people through the sermon, can be the means for beginning the healing process, how it can transfigure the way we see our lives and salve some of the pain we experience as a result of the past, as well as in later times of crisis.

15   Maggie Ross, *Silence*, p.31ff.

Chapter 3

Preaching as pastoral teaching: The search for healing

A few weeks ago, during what is known in the liturgical year as 'ordinary time', our vicar preached the most extraordinary sermon. One of the things which came through very clearly in her sermon was that there is no point in God's time which we can think of as 'ordinary'. Every event, even the most insignificant is, in a sense, 'extraordinary'.

Events do not happen of themselves. Human beings have a hand in shaping them and thus in their consequences, good or bad. Our vicar based her sermon on Mya Brooks Welch's poem 'The touch of the master's hand' in which an old violin is held up for auction. The violin is deemed by the auctioneer to be basically worthless, until an old man steps forward and having gently wiped the bow draws from it a single perfect note.

The point of the sermon lay in the priceless worth, the extraordinariness, of every human being in the eyes of God, even if they are unaware of it, or unable to face it. Our worth, or worthiness, in the eyes of God is a universal truth. It is true for everyone, whoever they are and whatever their circumstances. All that is needed is the touch of the Master's hand for our true worth, which is the goodness God sees in us, to be revealed and for us to own that goodness. No one in God's created order is worthless.

I do not know why this sermon spoke so powerfully to so many people, although I think I know why it spoke to me. It was an epiphany. It was about something I have always known, but tend to recoil from when I am feeling particularly 'low', or preoccupied with things which absorb my attention in ways which also disrupt my inner life, my on-going life in God.

Empathy as Understanding

Sermons need to connect with people's life experience. The sermon I have just described connected with its listeners because the preacher knew her people. She knew them personally and she knew them as the body of Christ. The preacher needs to know the people she is speaking to even if she has never met them, as Christ knew those he spoke to and healed on the wayside. When it comes to preaching, the body of Christ is the body of people who we are addressing right now, people who suffer and rejoice, who weep and laugh, just as Christ did. Irrespective of where they happen to be, whether in a national cathedral, a university chapel, or a struggling parish church, their life experiences are caught up in his. So we can only engage with them truthfully when we understand them *in* and *through* Christ.

To understand people *through* Christ is central to communicating the good news of the Gospel. We learn this from the apostle Paul who frequently prefaces his teaching with the Greek word *dia*, meaning 'by' or 'through'. The word *dia* can be understood in one of a number of ways. It can signify 'agency', as the cause or means of whatever thought or action is being referred to. It can also be the 'means' whereby the grace bequeathed to us in the person of Jesus and in his abiding Spirit is at work in our lives and inspires our thinking and teaching. Where these translations play into our English rendering of a given text, *dia* can mean 'for the sake of', so conveying a reason or meaning to an idea which will ultimately link that particular line of thinking to the life experience of the listener, something which may only occur long after they have heard the sermon.

To understand people *in* Christ refers us back to the sermon as a place of encounter. The encounter takes place through the 'returning' I described in the last chapter in which people and preacher meet with God in a common revelatory understanding, and in love. This shared understanding is coloured by the individual experiences of all who are involved, both listeners and preacher. But the understanding is almost always implicit, rather than explicit. It is a matter of empathy rather than sympathy.

People will be drawn to a person who preaches with empathy because they will sense that he has known pain. Having known pain, he will be offering them something more than sympathy. To be sympathetic is to listen, but without really hearing, and to respond in a way which seldom conveys understanding. Sympathy alone does not elicit trust. To live and teach from empathy is to have known the pain of simply being oneself, a pain which is only properly learned from a life honed in the parched deserts and fertile plains of prayer, and we have to travel through both.

Part of the journey will involve getting to know and forgive our true self, the self from which we hide most of the time or which is obscured by our public *figura*. The other part consists in allowing ourselves to be taught by God's Spirit, specifically with regard to praying for others and to loving them. We cannot do this until we have met and forgiven our true self and come to terms with our often conflicted emotions about other people, especially those we love. This is the foundation stone for intercessory discernment and the prayer which comes with it. It is central to the art of preaching.

Sermon preparation is a matter of waiting in the pain of others, rather than of worrying about what we are going to say. All Christians are called to this prayerful waiting, but it is the preacher's most important task and one which should occupy her at a subliminal level all of the time. This is not to say that she should be actively thinking of people in need to the exclusion of the rest of her normal life, but that she should 'bear' them within her, as a mother bears her unborn child. She should love them in the simple fact of their existence. In this way, she waits for the word of God to be born in her and to reveal itself in compassionate understanding. She does not simply worry about what she is going to say on Sunday, although I know from personal experience that this is what happens much of the time.

Men are also bearers of the word. They are called to take responsibility for the as yet unborn word of God by focusing their desire on it and by protecting it, as they think from the heart, and not with the mind alone. This, too, is a form of waiting. It requires that they resist the temptation to rationalise, order, plan and control. Instead, they must be patient. If they intellectualise the pre-nascent word too quickly, they will be honing their wits on the word of God which is as yet not fully formed in them. It is a dangerous thing for any preacher to do.

Both of the states of mind and heart which I have described form the basis of the kind of intercessory 'waiting' prayer which preachers need to be doing if they are to hear the truth as an epiphany, not only for those listening but first, and perhaps most importantly, for themselves. They will understand this truth instantaneously, in the briefest of passing moments, but they will not seek to control or hold it. They will not even try to remember it. Instead, they will consider the situations which some of their hearers might be experiencing at this present time, or one which affects the community.

Compassion

It is often the more general situation which elicits the compassion needed for a sermon to touch the individual in the moment. As I write, towns and villages in Great Britain have been devastated by winter flooding. When I preach this Sunday, I will want to connect whatever I say with this subject, although the text may only permit me to touch on it lightly. I will want to preach healing, even if I live in an area which has not been directly affected by this disaster. I will therefore spend the week engaging at the heart-mind level with those who are immediately affected by it. I will wait with them in it. In order to do this, I must keep up with the news as it unfolds on television and online. And I must also read newspapers, because the printed word is ingested in a different way. The printed word allows time for the rational and the intuitive to connect and make sense in ways which television and browsing the internet cannot.

As I sense the beginnings of a truth emerging from events, I try to engage with the individual suffering of those who are caught up in them. What does it feel like to have lost a house, or a business, when one is un-insured? The preacher will need to dwell on this question, not with the mind by working out practical ways with which to deal with this monumental problem, but with the 'deep mind'.[1] It is only at the level of deep mind that he is able to be in solidarity with the pain of the world[2] and, at the same time, in solidarity with the perhaps unknown pain of the persons he will be speaking to on Sunday.

The preacher will not, and may never, know how the pain of the world and whatever she has said about it connects with any one person who is suffering. But her own 'holding' of collective suffering in a given set of circumstances (flooding, for example) will make it possible for her words to kindle compassion, or bring inner healing to someone who could be suffering in an entirely different way. The person who is undergoing chemo will hear compassion for his own situation through the compassion spoken through (or *dia*) the preacher. It is not the person preaching who does the work of healing. It is the abiding Spirit of Christ who is 'working' and speaking through her.

1   See Chapter 2, note 4.
2   For a more extensive discussion of what this means see Whitehead & Whitehead, *Nourishing the Spirit*, p.132ff.

The work of healing

The idea of preaching as healing *work* is central to the art itself. It also makes the preacher's task part of a wider intercessory ministry. Speaking healing through a sermon becomes prayer. The healing work of preaching is the work of the Spirit, but it is also 'felt', like physical healing, in the listener's hidden inner life in which she seeks to know and be known by God. The preacher's words will have the same effect on that person as the words spoken by Jesus to those who sought him out, whether privately or in crowded streets.

When Jesus heals the blind man by the side of the road, the healing is both physical and spiritual (John 9:1-12). He touches the man and he speaks to him, so bringing together the work of prayer with that of healing. After he has rubbed them with earth and spittle, he tells him to go and bathe his eyes. But the healing begins a moment or two earlier, in Christ's wordless knowing, in his deep compassion for the man. He also addresses the Pharisees and others nearby. He heals the man of his blindness, and he then uses the man's former blindness to speak of himself as the light of the world. In doing so, he obliges some of his listeners to consider the kind of spiritual darkness they inhabit. He is, as always, controversial. In this particular instance, he threatens the religious status quo, and hence the power base occupied by some of his listeners. He does this by suggesting that the man's blindness has nothing to do with sins he might have committed, or with the sins of his parents, and then, through the words of the healed man, by forcing the religious establishment to come to terms with its own blindness with regard to him and to the work he is sent to do.

Throughout the gospels, we are shown that the priority for Jesus was not the fine tuning of words, or the display of knowledge, but that knowledge and words are given by God for the purpose of healing and forgiving God's people. This has immediate implications for the preaching ministry.

In his book, *Re-Enchanting Christianity*, Dave Tomlinson writes that 'practice is the touchstone against which Christology's authenticity has to be tested'.[3] He is describing an incident in the life of Mahatma Gandhi when the latter considered becoming a Christian but was put off the idea by the attitudes of Christians he met in the church he visited. Tomlinson is talking about the way Christians can come across when they are confident that they are the sole purveyors of religious truth. Preachers need to be wary of falling into a similar trap. A sermon and the public *figura* of the one preaching, as well as of others leading a service, can intimidate before anyone has said anything. Unqualified and unconditional love must be the first thing anyone experiences when they step through the door of a church. This is especially true for those who we know are experiencing any kind of trauma. People who have suffered loss or bereavement and who are coming to church, perhaps for the first time, can feel intimidated by their surroundings, by other people in the congregation and possibly by the sermon. So the preacher needs to be wary of preaching a sermon which may do unintended damage, especially if she does not know the congregation, or the individuals, personally. If she has

---

3   Dave Tomlinson, *Re-Enchanting Christianity* (Norwich: Canterbury Press, 2008), p.45.

waited on them with compassion during the preceding week, this is less likely to happen.

Healing without hurting

Here there is a paradox; the person preaching needs to be alert to the pain around her. There is always pain somewhere in the congregation. At the same time she must not worry too much about who will be there, or of causing offence by saying things which do not sit comfortably with the theology of a particular churchmanship. If she is vulnerable to the love of God, and wary of spirit, she is unlikely to fall into these traps. But if she has spent all week preparing a well-crafted sermon it is likely that, in the process, she will have lost touch with her listeners before she even begins to preach. It will have become *her* sermon. When it comes to pain and loss, the carefully honed sermon can alienate and even hurt people who are experiencing trauma, even if its subject has nothing to do with the circumstances in question, and especially if it has a moral or 'converting' sub-agenda.

People who have experienced loss or bereavement, for example, will be especially sensitive to anything implying the need for stoicism in the face of adversity. This is not to say that such an idea does not have its place, but it needs to be qualified and tempered with compassionate wisdom. Dwelling on the different aspects of courage would be one way to do this. But even here, the preacher needs to be careful not to sound as if he is moralising. There must not be even a hint of judgment. Sounding judgmental is a trap we can all fall into, especially when comparing like with like, in the examples we cite on any given subject. So it is important for the preacher to wait on the word, on the still small voice guiding him from his own experience of loss, even as he speaks. Only then will he connect with the pain which might be hovering in the space below or around him. The preacher must never forget the existence of pain, because it will always be there in one form or another.

A meeting with grief

So the one who is preaching must convey the idea that healing which pertains to salvation is not a matter of having the right answers to questions about God and the human condition. Healing begins with recognising and encountering Christ through the voice and the face of another person beginning, perhaps, with the preacher. The person in the congregation who has been recently bereaved, or suffered the untimely loss of an animal they love, will experience healing in the voice of the one preaching and sense it in their tone and gestures. Conversely, the one preaching will sense the suffering Christ present in those who are listening. The sermon is given to the people through the preacher, so it is, in a sense, a part of who she is. Through the preacher, it conveys the mystery of faith, something which is inextricably bound to love and which embodies truth. We cannot preach about God unless we love and trust him. Those who love and trust God with the whole of their lives will speak truth to their listeners in such a way as to take all of us, both preacher and listener, to a different place when it comes to thinking about God and the Christian faith.

We see this happening in the story of the widow of Nain who is on her way to her son's funeral. (Luke 7:11-17) When

Jesus raises the widow's son, a small crowd surrounds him. They probably consist of the funeral cortege and a few curious bystanders. They are a mixed congregation, some grieving, some just curious. Nobody expects what happens next, so this moment is unlike other healing and raising stories in which Jesus is asked by a friend or relative of the deceased or sick person to intervene. In this case he takes the initiative.

The little crowd of bystanders are not untypical of a small to medium sized congregation in any church. They are a mixed group. Some have come to church because they are going through a time of crisis. Perhaps they have been recently bereaved. Others come because they are passing through the area and would normally go to church on a Sunday, although possibly a church of a different denomination. These will be curious, and perhaps especially attentive to the sermon. Others have come because it is their church and this is what they do on Sunday morning. Some of the people following the funeral which took place in Nain that day were locals. They knew the woman and her son. Some were close relatives and were grieving with the mother. Some were just passing through the area.

In this story, and against this mixed background, we see compassion at work, not in a sermon, but in the few words spoken by Jesus to the woman and in the response his words elicit from the crowd. We are told that Jesus has compassion for her because she is in desperate circumstances. He knows that a widow who is without a son or male family member to protect and provide for her will not survive. He tells her not to grieve. Again, the message is in the wordless knowing. We are also told that the crowd 'glorified God' and that talk

47

of Jesus spread throughout Judea. But while they thought of him as a prophet, one suspects that they also glimpsed something of God in him, something which they did not as yet have words for.

Something like this happens when people hear a sermon which they might later tell the preacher 'meant' something to them. It will have elicited prayer, even if that prayer is no more than a sigh which comes with recognising and owning the state of loss which the preacher is alluding to. The prayer, or the sigh of recognition, connects that person directly to the compassion of Christ, just as he connected with the sorrow of the mother who was walking beside her son's funeral bier.

In the sermon, and through the person delivering it, people will hear and see something of God. What they see will perhaps surprise them. The preacher may not look like the kind of clergy they are used to. He may be wearing formal robes, or he may be untidy or dishevelled and wearing jeans. Or perhaps the preacher is a woman and they do not hold with women preaching, but they are taken unawares by what she says and by her manner of speaking which is a reflection of the person she is. She will have challenged prejudice, not deliberately or in a provocative manner, but through her own integrity as a person, an integrity which she finds within her life in God. Both these preachers will have met their listeners in their grieving, even if they knew nothing of their listeners' circumstances.

Facing loss

What I have said about bereavement and the need to be spiritually alert when preaching also applies to other situations of loss. To lose a job, or even to be in the early stages of retirement, especially if it is unexpected and undesired, is to face loss and bereavement. To be told that one is redundant is to be told that our lives and our very existence no longer serve any useful purpose. The preacher will need to be aware of this particular kind of bereavement. He will need to have known something like it in his own life if he is to connect with the person in the congregation who has suffered loss through redundancy or unplanned retirement.

The same holds for other loss situations. Terminal relationship breakdown is now recognised as something that almost everyone will experience at some point in their lives, from the ending of a love affair, to painful and permanent separation from parents or children in later life. All separation is bereavement and every separation which has not been reconciled cries out for forgiveness and healing. The preacher needs to be aware of the unspoken cries for healing that emanate from those around her. She needs to speak into them, even if she does not know the people concerned, without being specific and without appearing to single out any one person in the congregation. No one person should feel that they are being singled out for attention, but every person should feel attended to.

Delivering and listening to a sermon is not a private exercise. It is always about connecting with people. We connect with people by listening 'under' them, first in prayer and then through the spoken word. To listen under someone is to sense their needs through the text at the level of prayer, and to be obedient to what we intuit in that process. The New Testament Greek word for obedience translates as 'listening under', discerning the spirit of what we are asked to be or do, rather than simply obeying orders. The person preaching will be listening both to God, through the Holy Spirit already at work in her, and listening 'under' God's people through that same Spirit. God's people are also her people because God has entrusted them to her, even if she is a visiting preacher and has never met them before. The preacher is there to bring God to his people, so that God can attend to their needs. So preaching is a two way process. We listen to God as we speak, knowing that we need him and we listen to the people we are speaking to, knowing that we need them too. We need their empathy. The sermon which grows out of this spirit of listening, of obedience to both God and his people, creates communion, what we call the communion of saints.

Inspired preaching

So the sermon will always be a place of encounter, where those who are present on a Sunday morning sense, through what the preacher says and through her general demeanour, that they are part of a *worshipping* community. Being a worshipping community requires that we 'reconfigure' how we see ourselves and each other. No longer are we an assortment of people who have come to church for any one of a number of reasons. We are a cohesive body, a communion of persons, which understands itself as here for the purpose of meeting and worshipping the living God.

To be a worshipping community is to be in communion with each other and with the wider Church.

Communion is about sharing directly in the dynamic love of the Trinity. This dynamic love is one of mutual giving and receiving, beautifully portrayed in the Rublev icon of the Holy Trinity. The icon depicts a Eucharistic activity which also translates metaphorically as taking in and breathing out the love of God, both individually and in communion. Taking in and breathing out the love of God is what we might also call 'in-spired' preaching and listening.

The sound-bite culture we now inhabit has led to a devaluing of the idea of inspiration. This is one of the reasons why ready-made sermons found online seldom connect with those who either preach or listen to them. Downloading does not allow for the kind of time and *disponibilité* needed for the deeper wisdom of God to penetrate the heart and mind and emerge later as food for the hungry spirit. God's wisdom requires gestation over time.

As preachers, we are conditioned to the idea that people have limited attention spans and do not want to think deeply about God, or about anything. In our own state of chronic impatience, we assume that all our listeners suffer from the same universal attention deficit disorder, when in fact it is more often the preacher herself who is the sufferer, because she has neither the time nor the spiritual resources to wait attentively for the word to gestate in her heart during the preceding week, to breathe it in, to 'in-spire' it, trusting that it will yield its fruits when the time is right. For the preacher, inspiration is about waiting and breathing in the word of God, through the Holy Spirit who abides in her and who is the energy which inspires her to speak.

The activity of the Holy Spirit in the heart is the engine which drives our theological thinking and leads to pastoral preaching. The Spirit 'enlivens' or 'animates' the speaker's mind.[4] But this energy will also be felt, both by the one preaching and by the listener, as the 'still small voice' speaking out of the whirlwind of life and its many distractions. It is the quiet voice of God's Wisdom and love. It should also be our default position, the one to whom we naturally return, as we centre into the silence we carry within us, whatever we are doing at any point of the day.

Maggie Ross describes this God orientated state of mind and heart as 'intent', a continual returning to a state of deep listening to God.[5] Inspiration, properly understood, can only come from this place of intent, of being at the disposition of the living word. So the speaker's listening is again a matter of *disponibilité*. To be *disponible* is not to be passive, as though we were called to wait like zombies for God to 'speak' through us. We are called to submit our *will* to him. The will is an active force. Those who preach must learn to wait in an active way, with the will and the heart fully engaged in God.

Our will is the full complement of the intellectual and conscious faculties which define us to ourselves and to the community, and in which we are known by God. So, as preachers, we are called to let go of what is false, of the

---

4   Donald Coggan argues that words describing the Holy Spirit as 'comforter' and 'advocate' no longer resonate with people's life experience. 'Animator' or 'awakener' are more appropriate words to describe the energy, or inspiring grace, imparted by God's Spirit, especially in the context of preaching. See *Preaching the Sacrament of the Word*, p.76.
5   Maggie Ross, 'playing the games of paradox' or 'the paradox of intent' in *Silence*, p.48 – 49.

way we would like to come across, and to question opinions that only serve to reinforce our public *figura*. Instead, we are called to attune our thinking and speaking to the mind of Christ, to what Christ is saying to us and to his people. Bearing the word, and taking responsibility for it, liberates us all into fellowship with God and with the world. We are not only addressing the little congregation before us. In bearing the word of God we are speaking into the world's need, and bringing our listeners with us, keeping company with them in their separate loneliness and in our shared concern for the world. Our speaking and our bearing of the word returns us with them to that place where all human experience is brought together in Christ.

Chapter 4

Preaching as public theology: God with us

'It is a fearful thing to fall into the hands of the living God' (Heb. 10:31), but it is especially fearful for one who is called to speak or act in God's name in the context of public worship. As preachers, we need to respect this fear. It is wholesome. We need to be grateful for it because it reminds us of our natural limitations, and of certain other limits which we must not presume to exceed. A healthy fear of God, in whose presence we stand as persons entrusted with his Word, steadies us in the knowledge that we belong to God most intimately. As we speak, we are his in body, mind and spirit. We also belong, for the duration of this particular sermon, to his people, so we also need to know ourselves and how people perceive us when we preach.

The one who preaches knows herself as a person to the extent that she knows that she belongs also to those to whom she is speaking. She is literally 'at their mercy', not because she fears being judged by them, but because they have been entrusted to her as valued and unique persons in the eyes of God. God is utterly for them. So she must risk all that she is, and all her giftedness, or lack of it, for their sake. This is vital for her emotional well-being and indeed for her survival as a preacher. Without a deep conviction of God's specific calling to us as preachers, wobbly vessels that we are, we quake before the very thought of being bearers of the sacramental Word into the world, but this is what every preacher is called to be. We are called to be God's emissaries.

We are commissioned by God to speak his truth, his righteousness, into a world which often confuses truth with propositional certainties, or with current thought trends. 'Modernity is trying to sell us a bill of goods; it has truncated our sense of truth and warped our sense of wisdom', writes the philosopher, John Caputo.[1] Good religion, and good preaching, seeks to heal this deep collective psychic damage. For this reason, we do not pronounce dogmatic certainties, or curry intellectual favour with anyone. Instead, we remain focused on the abiding Spirit of Christ within us, waiting for the Word to reveal itself. We sense God's Word from our involvement with the world, in the ordinary business of life, and in all created matter. Part of our task is to speak that Word as blessing and sacrament.

Preaching is a sacramental act. It hallows the human and sometimes mundane thoughts which come even as the preacher is speaking. She will recognise the word, even as she sifts through her own distractions. It is God's word for his people. She has lived with it for the past week, in her own life in God, and sensed its meaning in the ordinary and the everyday. These initially vague connections, the relationship between what we see as ordinary and the extraordinariness

---

1   John D. Caputo, *Truth: Philosophy in Transit*, (London: Penguin, 2013), p.53.

of what is perceived in a single moment, will crystallise into spoken words when the time is right.

The sacramental Word proceeds from God and transfigures whoever it touches, whoever hears it. It changes the way they think of God, of themselves and of others. They will see things in a new light, a new radiance.[2] The sacramental Word transfigures both speaker and hearer, in the moment of speaking and in the manner in which it is heard. Each person will hear the Word, as the people in the street did on the morning of Pentecost, 'in their own tongue', filtered through their particular thought language. The language they hear will also be what is spoken by the person preaching. It will resonate with their present circumstances, or with some incident from the past. They will hear and understand what is being said in the way a person who speaks another language fluently 'understands' the mind of the speaker. This may yield surprises, as I have found when people share their particular understanding of what was said in the sermon, which is often quite different from anything I had thought I was saying. Their understanding is a revelation. It teaches me something. It is part of the three-way sermon dialogue which takes place between Christ, his people and the person preaching.

Both preacher and listener will understand, in their particular thought language, the mind of Christ. How a person understands is shaped by a person's context and by what they bring of their own sometimes unacknowledged feelings on any given subject. All of our lives will have been

---

2   *Writing the Icon of the Heart*, 'Cranberries', especially pp.17 - 18.

shaped by the society and culture of which we are a part. What the preacher says will resonate and strike a particular chord with how his listeners think about the world and the politics which shape their lives. The language they are hearing may also change perceptions, or heighten them, effecting a 'transfiguring'.[3]

The prophetic task and the sacramental Word

What is given to the preacher to say will reveal a much-needed new reality, a new truth. The arrival of the digital age, and the constant appeal to statistics, has brought with it an excessive amount of information. Excessive information obscures deep truth, so making effective communication difficult, if not impossible. Political pundits of all persuasions are particularly good at this kind of pseudo communication. They leave the reader or listener 'informed' but somehow disempowered.

The sacramental Word spoken through (*dia*) the preacher, out of her inner silence, does not disempower its hearers. It clears a space in which the deeper truth of God can be heard. The Word that is given to the preacher does not return to God empty. It returns bearing something of the listeners, something of the truth with which they have connected. So the preached Word is both sacramental and prophetic. It effects an encounter with God and returns to God as hallowed 'matter'. It will have been hallowed in a sensed three-way connection between Christ, the preacher and those

3   *Ibid.*

listening to her. What the preacher says will connect at the deepest level with the lives of her listeners, and with their particular areas of concern in regard to the politics of the day and world events. The sacramental Word transfigures these concerns into 'hallowed matter'. It takes them into the love of God.

The 'matter' in question is constitutive of the world we live in, as well as of our immediate surroundings and local community. The sacramental Word is the Word made flesh who is 'the true light which enlightens everyone' and who came into the world (John 1:9). The one who preaches is entrusted with the Word who comes into the society we live in, and who desires to heal it, so it is the preacher's task to make sense of the mystery of human destiny, the reason and purpose of human life, to create a 'grammar' which communicates God to the collective psyche and to do so in the space of a few minutes. The preacher is concerned with eternity and with the coming of the Kingdom. He must 'articulate our lives through the grammar of history, to discover those points at which the truth from beyond time has revealed itself at the heart of time'[4] He must tell God's people a story which connects the present moment with eternity, a story which is unfolding in the very moment of his speaking, and of their listening.

We learn in childhood that stories captivate their audience, whether they are read aloud, recounted, or read privately. When it comes to preaching, we are entrusted with the story of salvation, the story of God with us, as it is told in the

---

4   Roger Lundin, *Believing Again: Doubt and Faith in a Secular Age* (Grand Rapids: Eerdmans, 2009), p.23.

Bible. The story is a 're-figured' understanding of history and society in the light of God's being and activity in the world. How this idea of God's involvement with his world is conveyed by the preacher, and received by his listeners, will depend on how the preacher reads Scripture and does his theology. He must do it from a 'heart listening' place because theology is generated from that place. It is the poetry of God's activity in the world.[5]

The stories Jesus told were parables, or poetic metaphors, which he either adapted or turned around in order to teach his listeners something new. The stories themselves may have been already familiar to them, which made the moral all the more disturbing and perhaps subversive. But Jesus was also concerned with how these parables were heard; whether they helped people to better understand the signs of the times. Preaching is prophetic because it reads the signs of the present times with the mind of Christ, rather than predicting the future through a particular political or theological lens.

Preachers often find themselves in a lose-lose situation when it comes to how their prophetic task is viewed. They will either be told not to mix religion with politics, or they will be criticised for not being 'relevant'. Both these accusations ignore the meaning and purpose of the prophetic task of preaching. Religion has always been about God's ways with the world, about his on-going relationship with human beings, and hence about politics.

Relevance is too often confused with whatever is 'trending'. Trend, like information, seldom penetrates

---

5   See Daniel W. Hardy, *God's Ways with the World: Thinking and Practising Christian Faith* (Edinburgh: T&T Clark, 1996), especially Chapter 5.

beyond the surface of the world's pain, fear and need. The preacher, as emissary, is 'commissioned' by God to speak the truth of the Gospel *into* that pain and fear, to go below the surface. This obliges her to think beyond relevance and to be circumspect about her own political views. She is not to use the preaching task as a platform on which to drum up support for a particular party line, or for her own position on any given issue. She is called to be present to the world's pain and need, so that she can speak the truth into it. Discretion will bring vital humility to this task.

When we preach about the goodness in the world, we will often be accused of pandering to secularism, or of trying too hard to be relevant. Both these terms, spoken as an accusation, amount to a blanket definition in the minds of many people for everything which does not sit well with what the Bible appears to teach. Discomfiting newness is also written off as the pernicious work of secularism, itself 'a code for unwelcome social change'.[6] But secularism, or 'the spirit of the age', also embodies the truth of the gospel. In the introduction to his book *The Soul of Doubt*, Dominic Erdozain argues that secularism, or 'the dichotomy between "religious" and "secular" thought, is unsustainable'. Secularism and Christian apologetics 'share a common root system'.[7] The preacher needs to be deeply convinced of this fact and that the love and mercy of God are at work in the world, regardless of what systems do to the human spirit

---

6   See Dominic Erdozain, *The Soul of Doubt: The Religious Roots of Unbelief from Luther to Marx* (Oxford: OUP, 2016), Introduction.
7   *Ibid.*

and of what a systemised Church has done to the Christian religion.

The preacher is concerned with this dichotomy, the dichotomy that exists between the religious and the secular. His task is not to subject the secular to God by simply condemning it. That would be inherently judgmental and theologically suspect. The judgment of God is not about condemnation and spurious conquest. It is about wisdom and compassion. The preacher's task is to discern the wisdom of God at work in the world and in the Church. By wisdom we mean the dynamic activity of God, which is fuelled by love and known, or revealed, in his Spirit. (John 16:13) These ideas challenge and constrain the preacher, whatever the present circumstances, and whatever the text of the day, because if he is to communicate them in a way which is truthful, he must be open to the 'convicting' of the Spirit. He must be obedient to God's loving purpose, wherever it is made plain to him. This may lead him down surprising paths. He will almost certainly challenge his listeners.

Some months ago, following another murderous attack by the so called Islamic State terrorist group, I invited the congregation to consider the Isis murderer as a man who had once been a child, a baby. The boy, and now the man, is someone's son, someone's grandchild. He has known love in his life. Without proposing an answer, I invited them to wonder what it was that had made him as he is today and, in doing so, to remember that evil is not only a spiritual force at work in the world, but that it lodges itself in the human heart, is shaped in the human mind and purposed through human will. The sermon was delivered in two different churches on the same morning. The reactions were polarised.

Some people went away angry at the suggestion that an Isis murderer could still have the potential for love and goodness, despite having chosen to do such evil. Others reacted in a quite different way. The sermon had been, in every sense, controversial.

When Jesus spoke to people he was not trying to be controversial in order to create a sensation. He was controversial to the extent that he invited people to change the way they saw things and, in so doing, to be changed in themselves. This was his 'judgment' and it continues to be effected through good preaching. The preacher must therefore discern where the judgment lies through the reading of any text. He does not come to the text with ready made decisions. He does not pre-judge, even though he may be outraged and saddened by cruelty and injustice. Instead, he takes the righteous anger that he feels into his inner silence and lives with it while waiting on the word that he will be given. He may be surprised by what he says when the moment comes for him to speak.

Speaking hope into the world

He may be surprised by a sudden interruption of hope. During the preceding week, the preacher, like everyone else, will have been wondering what there is left to hope for, given the state of the world. What can he possibly have to say to a group of people who are looking to the Church to be a light to the nations? He knows that he is not expected to provide answers, but he also senses that people look to him to lighten their darkness in some way.

There is no prescribed method for doing this. Love and faith will suffice, as Scripture repeatedly tells us. They are the substance, the raw material, from which the sermon will emerge, like clay which in its crude initial state already suggests the shape of the figure which the sculptor is trying to release. The clay has to be handled in a particular way. Prophetic preaching requires that we also handle text in a particular way, with the inward eye of love and faith, and that we love the people listening to us with ordinary human affection, as Jesus did. We see them and the world through the eyes of Christ.

Seeing the world through the eyes of Christ means having compassion for all who are caught up in the world's evil, beginning with the jihadi who was once a child, but who now rapes and terrorises women and girls and conscripts children, and ending with the people sitting in front of us. All of them, and the preacher herself, are caught up in the events of our times while being held in the eternal and unrelenting embrace of God. The person preaching will be caught up in God's embrace from the moment she begins to speak. She may have already known its force, and at times resisted it.

God's embrace is forceful. It grips us even when, like awkward adolescents, we pull away from it. I witnessed something like this at a neighbouring table in a Greek taverna, when we were on holiday. The extended family were all present, it being Sunday, and there was a friendly but quite heated altercation between the father and his adolescent son. The boy lost the argument. As they left the table, the father kissed his son on both cheeks and then locked him in a fierce paternal hug, from which the boy initially struggled, but eventually yielded to. It was a father's love, tactile, full of passionate empathy for what his son was feeling at that moment. We need to have known something like this in our relationships with our children and parents if we are to understand what God's passionate embrace says about his ways with the world and correct some of the mistaken ideas we have about his 'wrath'.[8]

Speaking love and hope into violence

God's passionate embrace is the measure of what the Bible calls his wrath. It is the wrath of divine love in the face of violence. Violence is all that we do to mar his image in others, in our world and in ourselves. God's wrath is never anything other than love. We feel its passion through Christ and it works in us as we preach, especially when we invite people to think about the politics of the day. We 'embrace' those listening to us with the loving embrace of God as we invite them to reflect on the world's sin and pain. God's wrath has little to do with anger (I do not think that God feels anger in the way we feel it) but it has everything to do with grief, grief about sin.

The judgment which accompanies wrath is worked in Christ's death and rising. In Christ, the love of God embraces our hopelessness, in the face of so much destruction, and makes of it a new creation. Hopelessness becomes the stuff of hope itself. Giovanni Bellini's painting of the risen Christ, *Christ Blessing*, shows us this hope in the simplicity of the

---

8   For a fuller discussion of the wrath of God, in the context of atonement, see my *Making Sense of God's Love: Atonement and Redemption* (London: SPCK, 2011), Chapter 3.

gesture of greeting, in the unwavering love of the face, in the vulnerability of the body. The words we speak need to do the same. They must convey unwavering love and hope, love which does not have highs and lows, but which is steady, even unprepossessing and ordinary and which comes, in some measure at least, from our own vulnerability. Only then will our preaching return us to the central message of the Gospel, to that epiphany, that truth which is already known. Only then will we, who will have known hopelessness in one form or another, preach hope into the lives of others.

Speaking hope into hopelessness

When I was a child I was often told I was 'hopeless'. It was probably not meant unkindly. It was simply unthinking, so I tried to see it as no more than affectionate teasing. In any case, the word was common parlance among children then (especially girls) as well as among adults. It was also a class identity marker. At boarding school you could be called 'hopeless' at maths or games and this would undermine your self-confidence with the result that you became 'hopeless' at joining in and were consequently marked as lacking 'team spirit', and thereby 'hopeless'.

If you are put down in anyone's book as hopeless, the idea follows you into adult life. You are, in a sense, written off, so you become hopeless to yourself. This sense of one's own hopelessness, and the need to prove everyone wrong about how we believe we are perceived, lingers on in all sorts of guises, including the need to succeed at all costs. Sometimes a person's sense of hopelessness is so well disguised as to be unrecognisable until that person hits a crisis in their life which has been provoked by some kind of failure linked to material achievement. While hopelessness may be felt privately, perhaps in the kind of loss I described in the last chapter, it also has a very public face.

We deal with hopelessness, and sometimes experience it as well, through the superficial, the material and the counterfeit. Hopelessness obliges us to put on a *figura*. The person preaching will know this, especially if their lives have taken them to places and situations of hopelessness, where they perhaps have lived for long periods in a material wilderness of one kind or another, trying to be someone they were never meant to be, presenting a brave face to the world. The truth about the central message of the Gospel is not that our lives are magically transformed because we have found God, but because all our life experience, especially the suffering which comes with hopelessness, is re-worked in us into a new thing, a new creation. There is no more need for the brave face. As preachers, we need to have known the re-working of our own hopelessness if we are to convey this idea as truth for the people who listen to us, whose lives may be in need of such re-working.

Their lives, like ours, are part of the wider context of human suffering, so whatever is being re-worked in them must also be re-worked in the world of which we are all a part. The preacher is there to invite reflection on how this is already being done, and possibly to suggest practical ways for the worshipping community to enter into this re-creative work. But inspired preaching will do more than encourage activity, especially when that activity, though well meant, does not address the root cause of suffering, or the primary needs of those who suffer.

What we are seeing in the refugee camp in Calais at this present time is not the kind of re-working promised by Christ, even though intentions are often for the best. Local churches and communities are doing what they can to alleviate immediate suffering, but the tents are still there and so are the people. What is needed is a change of heart in the way we, as a nation, think about other human beings and the situation which caused them to be refugees in the first place, for which we, as a nation, are partly responsible. Then the re-working can begin.

The preacher's prophetic task begins with helping the worshipping community to experience this change of heart. His task is to help his listeners connect with history, and thereby take responsibility for the politics of the day, while at the same time knowing the passionate love of God which is at work in history and in the present moment, even as he speaks. 'The "Spirit" is not a personal God who reigns over history, but a cosmic force that emerges from within it'[9] in the present moment. The preacher's own life will be rooted in this force, in the dynamic life of the Spirit, which is the abiding presence of Christ within him and which ties him to others. His own life and his teaching will therefore derive from God, from his deepening relationship with the God who is the source of hope for the world and for our lives.[10]

Through whatever text we are using we are conveying the reality of Emanuel, God with us. This reality is both in

---

9   *Believing Again*, p.18 (G.W.F. Hegel, quoted in Charles Taylor, *Hegel and Modern Society*, Cambridge University Press, 1979 p. 96).

10   See David E. Jenkins, *God, Jesus and Life in the Spirit*, SCM, London (1988) especially Chapter 3 'Towards a renewal of mysticism and politics'.

the present moment and, simultaneously, in times past and future. As preachers, we live our lives in the 'now and the not yet',[11] in a past brought into the present and manifested through us as hope in the future. We speak into the present as we encounter and work out, in our lives and teaching, the truth of God's being with us and for us, as we 'discover those points at which the truth from beyond time has revealed itself at the heart of time.'[12]

The heart of time is in the moment of Christ's rising, which is the definitive sign of hope for the world, focused in the present day, in and through whatever is happening in the world and in our lives. We sense this hope in our continued life in Christ and we convey it in our manner of speaking as well as in what we actually say. This is especially important with regard to contentious texts and the issues which they raise.[13] Dealing with contentious issues is not only a matter of exegetics. We first need to face whatever is going on in our own hearts and minds with regard to any one issue, our own anger, pain, or just plain bewilderment. We also need to be constantly aware that we do not have the ultimate solution to injustice or to how to resolve its long term consequences.

Speaking hope into contentious issues

The two areas of injustice which are currently diminishing the life of the Church concern the honouring of women,

---

11   I owe this description of the meaning of what is technically known as realised eschatology to a sermon preached by Jeremy Begbie at Ridley Hall, Cambridge.

12   *Believing Again*, p.23.

13   See Chapter 6.

and the honouring of gay and transgendered people. To honour someone is not only a matter of bestowing awards and status. It is not even about 'acceptance', a vague term which has come to mean very little. It is about acknowledging human worth and giving hope.[14] This involves vulnerability, which is our response to the naked vulnerability of Christ, as we see him in the Bellini painting. In being vulnerable to others at this deep and personal level, we take that person or group with us into the open embrace of God, 'the dynamic relationship between the self and the other' that 'symbolizes and acts' forgiveness and we allow them to do the same for us.[15] This is the cutting edge of acceptance. It begins in a deep and *mutual* acceptance of the love of God, of his passionate embrace. We cannot get out of the existing impasse in the Church unless we all fully and openly acknowledge our need for God, and for his love, and unless we embrace one another at this level.

This is, in part at least, the message of the story which Jesus told about the man who sold all his land in order to buy a single pearl.(Matt.13:45) His need was so great that he sacrificed everything he valued in order to pick up the pearl he so coveted. In the life of the Church, when we truly know our need for God we will stop at nothing for that need to be met. This will involve embracing those we fear and sometimes asking for their forgiveness. So we shall have to

14 David E. Jenkins, *God, Jesus and Life in the Spirit*, Chapter 3.
15 See Miroslav Volf, *Exclusion and Embrace: A Theological Exploration of Identity, Otherness and Reconciliation* (Nashville, Abingdon Press, 1996), especially Chapter 3 'The Drama of Embrace' p.141ff. For more on honour as merit and reward see my blog post of 30 December, 2015 http://jobbingtheologian.blogspot.co.uk/2015/12/love-bravely-in-2016.html.

put down what is 'valuable', what 'protects' us from them, in order to pick up the pearl of great price which is the love of God reached through persons who we fear because we do not understand them.

Fear, in most cases, is evidenced in the kind of protective measures we deploy in regard to people who we do not fully understand. In the case of the exclusion and diminishment of both women and gays in the life of the Church, fear derives from ancient and still only partially acknowledged taboos relating to sexuality and, in the case of interaction between women and men, the ever present dominating ethos of the alpha male, now shared in almost equal measure by a good number of women. Both women and men share the same fear of people they do not understand, especially when they themselves want power, and both women and men protect themselves from those they fear through whatever power they already have. When it is naturally theirs, by virtue of intellect or personal charisma, it evokes envy. As with the world, so with the Church.

Power, in all its forms, is addictive. As I said earlier,[16] anyone who preaches will, at some point in their preaching ministry, have known power, the 'hold' which they exercise on their listeners when they preach from within their own life in God, and this returns us to the beginning of this chapter. We need to feel the right kind of fear in regard to what is given to us to say in the moment of preaching. If we do not feel this fear, we will abuse our power and risk abusing our listeners. For the preacher, the right kind of

16   See Chapter 1.

fear comes with an abiding but awe-filled love for God, the kind which Scripture attributes to angels and prophets. At the beginning of the book of Isaiah we read of angels who worship in adoration, of the prophet who receives the touch of a burning coal on his lips when he implores God to send him as his emissary (Isaiah 6).

In the light of such imagery, the issues which may come up on a Sunday morning, as well as those which currently preoccupy the Church, become something more than 'issues'. They reflect the concerns of God. The preacher is nothing less than an emissary sent by God to convey these concerns to his people and to be an agent for the transforming, or re-working, of the minds of all who are present, including the mind of the preacher. If the sermon has grown out of the silence of 'beholding', it will transfigure both listener and speaker together.[17] Only when the preacher allows for this deep understanding of how things stand between God, the world and his people, and the transfiguring which comes with it, will she truly communicate God's Word.

---

17   See Maggie Ross, *Writing the Icon of the Heart*, 'Liturgy in truth' p.61. The beholding of God is central to Ross's thinking. See especially her essay 'Barking at Angels', p.19ff.

Chapter 5

Becoming an effective communicator: The preacher as Connector

Shortly after his election, Pope Francis gave a press interview. Eugenio Scalfari, the co-founder of the Italian newspaper *La Reppublica*, and a declared atheist, asked the Pope whether he believed that salvation was intended solely for Catholics. Pope Francis replied 'I believe in God, not in a Catholic God. There is no Catholic God. There is God and I believe in Jesus Christ, his incarnation'.[1]

There is no Catholic God, and there is no Anglican God, or Methodist, or Evangelical God of any hue or persuasion. There is only God and his Christ, and Christ is for everyone, including atheists. The preacher is called to be an emissary for that God and to embody Christ for everyone, beginning with the people sitting in front of her on a Sunday morning. She embodies Christ through her speaking. Her speaking will proceed from her knowledge of her own uniqueness and value in the eyes of God and it will have been shaped

---

1   http://www.bbc.co.uk/news/world-europe-30899671.

by the inevitable pain, as well as delight, of becoming fully
the person she is.

Given that all people belong to God, whether or not they
think of themselves as religious, the preacher must know
that the people he is addressing *already* belong to the God of
whom the Pope was speaking. The preacher will be speaking
to people who may know God better than he does. His task
is therefore to connect with his listeners by making it possible
for them to connect with, or meet for the first time, someone
who has known them for the whole of their lives.

In order to do this, he must also know that the people he
is speaking to are his own 'kin', because they belong with him
in God. The institutional Church, and its preoccupation with
status-defined identity, obstructs the vital sense of kinship
which ought to bind the preacher to his listeners. It does so on
two fronts; first because an increasingly managerial approach
to ministry and to the life of the Church separates people
from one another and from their pastors and preachers.
The Church is increasingly seen as an organisation rather
than as God's beloved people. This inhibits trust because
you cannot love an organisation. You can only love people.
Second, because an organisation is inevitably self-serving
and self-aggrandizing. Its success depends on growth. To
this end, the Church promotes quantifying agendas which
diminish the true value of God's people and obscures him
from their eyes. This has the effect of devaluing worship
itself. People become numbers, with ministry and worship
increasingly 'rated' in terms of maintaining and justifying
the existence of buildings and, to this end (which is seldom
acknowledged), promoting growth as 'mission'. None of

these scenarios have anything to do with the knowledge of God, or with genuine kinship.

The knowledge of God, and the empathy which will naturally spring from it, requires that the preacher arrive at a kind of certainty of the heart. This is not an intellectual certainty. It is a certainty which comes from having thought deeply about, or 'contemplated', the events and circumstances of the birth, ministry, dying and rising of Jesus of Nazareth and, by doing so, knows and is known by God. Knowing that we are known by God can also be felt as a re-formative, or life changing, encounter, which can occur even in later life and in the most unlikely circumstances.

Encounter

Something like this happened to the director of the acclaimed BBC production, *The Nativity* (2010). The director, Tony Jordan, was also the lead writer for *East Enders*. He was no stranger to the realities of modern life and he wanted this short series, which would be aired in the run-up to Christmas, to be equally hard-edged and relevant. He met and talked with people of faith. He also met with historians and scientists, who were largely convinced that the nativity story was folk lore, an expanded compilation of the details of an ordinary event, handed down through several generations by word of mouth. For many people today, the Christmas story is still folk lore. But Jordan sensed there was more to it. So he began to ask himself questions about the key players. He wanted to meet them. At some point in the filming of the birth itself he had an epiphany moment when he *knew* that the event was true, not only historically but in a profound and life changing sense. Somewhere in the directing process, he had 'met' the key players, Mary, Joseph, the shepherds, the Magi, and allowed himself to be known, or perhaps 'interrogated' by them. A kind of intuited dialogue would have begun in this encounter, the kind of dialogue which is vital to genuine communication.

The preacher is on a similar journey. He will have met Christ. Meeting Christ is not a matter of mastering the techniques of meditation. Meditation techniques are useful as a means to an end, but they can also obstruct the very end for which they are purposed by becoming an end in themselves and thereby a cause of anxiety. Anxiety endangers the dynamic of prayer by diverting it back to the self without the person who is doing the meditating necessarily realising that this is what is happening. When technique becomes an end in itself it interferes with the two-way communication, or dialogue, which God so desires to have with us. It can also inhibit surprise. To be known by God, to arrive at the kind of conviction which Tony Jordan experienced, is to be taken by surprise. In the simplicity of the moment of encounter and *knowing* we also know that we have something precious to communicate, as Tony Jordan did. Being faithful to this knowledge, trusting in its truth, disposes us to communicate it effectively. This is why the *The Nativity* was so moving and so powerful.

Simplicity is the essence of true communication. By simplicity I mean being humble in our handling of the truth as it is revealed to us in the two-way activity of prayer and in the contemplative study of Scripture and theology. Simplicity is not about talking down to people by patronising or manipulating them. It is about humility of mind and heart.

Together, these allow us to perceive the Christian faith in a new light, as it pertains to the human condition in the world of today. The truth we are dealing with is not a set of propositions leading to contentious arguments. Neither is it an abstract philosophical ideal with which we are to somehow excite people. The truth is already present in the hearts of those listening to the sermon, waiting for the preacher to awaken it into life. Somewhere, between the expression of an opinion and the putting forward of an argument, we have communication of a truth which pertains to the love of God.

Communicating God

Preachers are concerned with communicating a truth which takes them beyond words and beyond the rational process itself. They speak out of the expectant silence of the heart. Their listeners wait with mind and heart for the word with which both preachers and listeners engage together. The Word changes all of us in the simplicity of a single moment. It changes our perspective on God and on what it means to be human. It 'transfigures' how we think and thereby transfigures the understanding of those listening to us. This is what happened to Tony Jordan and what must have happened to many of those who watched *The Nativity*.

As preachers, we are called to enliven the imagination of those we speak to through our own transfigured understanding of the truth and through our knowing and being known by God. It is this quiet confidence which makes it possible for our listeners to encounter Jesus Christ as we speak, or when our words come to their minds at some later time.[2] Our own encounter with Christ is therefore central to the work of evangelism. The preacher engages people by being a certain kind of person, one who is quietly but deeply confident that she is loved by God and that she is tasked with preaching his word. If the preacher is unsure about herself, or anxious about her status in the institutional Church, or whether she is really loved and accepted by the community she serves, she will not be able to convince people of the truth that she is proclaiming. This is not because she has failed as a preacher, but because she may not have adequately maintained her deep connection with Christ. If we are to re-awaken the imagination of our listeners, we need to connect with them in a way which corresponds to the way we connect with Christ. We hold them by 'intent' in our 'beholding' of him at all other times and in all other places.[3] Other preoccupations obstruct that connection.

There is a world of difference between truth that has been re-awakened by an imagination which comes of knowing and being known by God, and the duplicitous imagination of advertising and various kinds of socio-political, as well as religious, propaganda machines. Preaching is not about propaganda. It is about telling the good news of the Gospel; that we are unconditionally loved by God and that there is nothing we can do or say to alter this central truth, although there will always be pain and suffering in coming to terms with it.

2   James A. Wallace, *Preaching to the Hungers of the Heart* (Collegeville: Liturgical Press, 2001), p. 87

3   See Maggie Ross, *Writing the Icon of the Heart*, 'Cranberries' p.18. (For more on the word 'intent' see note 5 Chapter 3.)

Receiving the love of God requires that we strip ourselves of illusions. Receiving the love of God also entails passing it on to others, whatever the cost. Evangelism consists in proclaiming this central truth from which all other truths will follow. The preacher will be gifted with the kind of imagination needed to connect people with the truth of God's unconditional love for all human beings, so she must be true to her commission, even at the risk of sounding controversial, as I sounded when I suggested there might once have been, and may yet be, something lovable in the Jihadist.

The 'What if?' question

Connecting with our listeners from that inner 'place' where we encounter Christ gives us immense freedom. Maintaining our own prayerful connection with God, in Christ and through God's on-going and abiding Spirit, allows us to ask what I would call the 'What if?' question. The 'What if?' question pertains to the intuitive realm of heart knowledge. We 'know these things are true', as St John did when he wrote his gospel, or when the prophet Job says 'I *know* that my redeemer lives'. This is knowledge of the heart, rather than of the intellect. We *know* a truth which pertains to something deeper than mere facts or propositions. We do not just believe it. Some writers call this knowing 'imagination'.[4] Sanctified imagination, or the Wisdom of the Holy Spirit,

---

4   See Kate Bruce, *Igniting the Heart: Preaching and Imagination,* (London: SCM, 2015), p. 19; and Kerry Dearborn, *Drinking from the Wells of New Creation: The Holy Spirit and the Imagination in Reconciliation* (Cambridge: James Clarke & Co., 2015), Chapter 2.

gives us permission to turn things around so that they reveal a new truth or insight.

Take, for example, the story of the Good Samaritan. The preacher will usually emphasise the plight of the person who has been mugged, the kindness of the passer-by and the trusting hospitality of the man who took him in. But what if we read it differently? Seldom do we hear very much about the two people who passed by on the other side of the road, despite the fact that they are highly significant. They represent the chronic loneliness which is a direct result of our indifference to the circumstances of other people, the protective self-interest so characteristic of our times, and of our busy and affluent western society. If we read this story in the context of the refugee crisis which is being played out on the beaches of northern France and on the barbed borders of an increasing number of other European countries, it becomes a grim prophetic warning about the future of Europe itself. Turning a blind eye to suffering, by refusing to work together as nations, will ultimately cause our own fragmentation. Without compassion, and a shared duty of care 'the centre cannot hold'.[5] The nations become like the two men who passed by on the other side – disconnected from each other, with no good deed that they can share and rejoice in. The European Union, which is failing to unite to do the practical work needed to alleviate human suffering on such a vast scale, may soon cease to have any reason at all to 'hold'.

5   W.B. Yeats, *The Second Coming*

The Good Samaritan story invites preachers to risk being political. But as I said in an earlier chapter, the preacher's mandate does not entitle her to promote her own party political preferences by pressing the advantage which the pulpit affords. This would be an abuse of her authority. She must always remember that she holds her authority from God in order to be a bearer of the Word into the lives of her listeners. They in turn will bear it into the world to the extent that it effects a transformation of their thinking on any number of issues. So preaching is a three-way listening dialogue. The preacher listens and waits for God's word for the world, *even as she is speaking*, and as she also intuits the people's thoughts and concerns. In doing this, she returns her listeners to God. Her listeners will intuit the word as an epiphany, so preaching is a three-way learning process, as the preacher will find when someone returns that epiphany to her later during coffee.

If preaching is also a learning process, for both preacher and listener, it begs a further question. What kind of God are we talking about when we preach? Consider, for example, the vexed question of why prayers are not always answered. Some will be wondering how it is that a good God can continue to allow bad things to happen to innocent people, especially children. What, then, do we mean when we say 'Thy will be done'? To them, the words sound more like submissive fatalism than prayer. Part of the preaching commission consists in allowing these difficult questions to surface. The key to addressing the 'What if?' question lies in encouraging the kind of creative questioning which leads to mature faith. The words 'Thy will be done' only sound like submissive fatalism when we imagine God as a kind of wizard who can be conjured up to perform magical acts at our behest. What if he were different? And how does that impact on our lives and on our priorities, or what we pray for?

Simple belief sustains simplistic thinking and leads the worshipping community down an intellectual dead end. Simple belief is not faith. This is why God invites questions, as he invited Job in his time of trial, and Jacob, who wrestled with an angel and was left a marked man. The freedom we are given to question God, and to wrestle with him spiritually and intellectually, builds trust, the sign of mature faith. The sermon is of special significance in this regard because part of the preacher's commission consists in bringing his listeners to mature faith. The preaching task is to educate as well as to console and exhort. The true meaning of education, a word derived from the Latin *educare*, is to 'lead forth', so the preacher must communicate the Word in a way which allows his listeners to mature in their understanding of God as well as of Christian discipleship. He must lead them from one place of understanding to another. As a result of this, they will learn that God is not an angry school master who is waiting for us to give wrong answers, but a God who loves the human mind and wishes us to trust him while also loving him with our intelligence, as the first commandment tells us.

Knowing self

Some people, especially those who have suffered emotional or physical trauma, will never have known trust and the healthy self-confidence which comes with it. The preacher needs to have the humility to know that such people will not suddenly discover the trust that comes with faith as a result of hearing her carefully prepared sermon, but that they may begin to get a feeling for it in the simplicity and absence of guile with which she puts it across, in her openness and vulnerability to their doubts and possible anger towards God.

Simplicity comes with self-forgiveness. The preacher will have looked at his life in all its complexity, and perhaps at his empty wasted years, and seen that his life, and those years especially, are rich and valuable to God. In doing this, he will learn to accept that his past is as it is and that it cannot be changed, so he must forgive it and allow God to work with him as he begins to see that past in a 'transfigured' light.[6] In doing this, he will learn that those supposedly wasted years were in fact the 'compost' of his later life, of his coming to faith and of his vocation as a preacher. They enriched it and made it fruitful from the moment he trusted God enough to allow his Spirit to work a new creation out of the past, so that God's will for the people to whom he is now speaking could be done through his preaching ministry.

We will not be effective communicators of God's loving purpose if we are not humbly confident that our own life is being worked to this purpose through our vocation as preachers. We speak from our own suffering, without referring to it directly, so that we can connect with the suffering of those who listen to us. Our listeners will sense that they are known and forgiven by God in the moment of our speaking, whatever the text. This overwhelming knowledge tempers any momentary feelings of vainglory.

6   See Chapter 2, p. 36, and note 15.

Instead, it reminds us of the weight of responsibility which we bear to God's people. What we say can make or break another person. It follows that as preachers we are answerable to God for the extent to which we have made them know that they are loved and accepted.

Gift

God's will for his people is that they should know the infinite height, length and breadth of God's love for them in Christ. His will is also that they, as well as the person preaching, should be confident about their own giftedness. If we do not know we are gifted, how can we possibly know we are loved? And how can we trust? Similarly, if we are not confident that God's people also love us and trust us, we will not be able to communicate to them God's living Word.

Knowing we are loved is not a matter of knowing that we are popular. Popularity is fickle. It can vanish overnight. But healthy self-confidence is a gift from God which the preacher needs to understand and claim in prayer. The same holds true for the gift of preaching. Understanding one's own giftedness begins with accepting it and then surrendering it to God, so that it can be tempered with discernment, self-awareness and gratitude.

Women often find it hard to acknowledge and be grateful for their giftedness. As I said in the last chapter, some of us are so conditioned to feeling that we are 'hopeless' that we would be at a loss to know how to live without this comforting and familiar falsehood. Ingrained hopelessness lets us off the hook when it comes to realising our full human potential. But when hopelessness is burned away from us by the refining fire of God's love, we are faced with who we really are and with the responsibility of nurturing and serving others with our giftedness.

The gift of prophetic preaching, the kind of preaching which reaches the hidden depths of the human heart, is a gift we need to ask for, even if we have never known what it feels like to have it. Here again, we need a combination of discernment and humility. Discernment should come from those who select and train people who are called to public ministry. Not everyone is called to preach, just as not everyone should be asked to sing solo in public if they do not have that particular gift. I found this out for myself, or rather my training incumbent did, when during my otherwise extremely happy curacy, I was told I had to sing choral evensong. The service was ruined by my efforts and, happily, I have not had to do it again. Nobody should be made to either preach or sing if, after prayerful discernment, it is clear that they do not have these particular gifts. However, there may be people who are not ordained to public ministry who do have them. It is everyone's responsibility to discern gift in others, irrespective of age, gender or status.

One way to begin to realise the giftedness of others, when it comes to preaching, would be to imagine the sermon itself in a quite different way. Sermons could be more like conversations, especially where congregations are small. Small country churches will often hold services in the choir or chancel section of the building rather than in the nave. This makes for a more intimate and sometimes warmer environment in which the acoustics are less challenging. In such a setting it will be easier for the person who is preaching to simply talk to the people, as Jesus did. If the preacher knows them personally, he might even invite response or comments as he speaks. I have known churches that have a time for questions built in to the service itself, either immediately after the sermon, or later during coffee. Allowing questions engages people. It also reinforces trust because in allowing questions the preacher empowers his listeners.

Jesus empowered his listeners as he taught them. He treated much of his teaching as dialogue. He would invite questions with the words 'How do you read?' Or he would challenge his questioner personally, as he did the rich and religiously observant young man, who wanted to know what more he needed to do to inherit eternal life. (Matt.19:16-22) In allowing the question Jesus challenged the young man to face the truth about himself; that he was captive to his own wealth and status and that true life and freedom come through dispossession. He also challenged his friend Nicodemus, a senior rabbi (possibly the equivalent of a bishop or archbishop in the Church of today), by suggesting that Nicodemus was spiritually blind. His spiritual blindness made all his theological knowledge seem childish, and the status that came with it irrelevant. Jesus also empowered ordinary people by allowing criticism. Some of their questions came in the form of resentful muttering: Who did this Jesus think he was, to lecture them? Was he not the local carpenter's son? Did they not see his mother and brothers every day of the week? Recognition of another's gift often takes the form of envy and aggression, even a kind of mute or implicit heckling.

Although we seldom experience heckling in church services these days,[7] resistance to what the preacher is saying, and resentment, even if it is not meant personally, can come across as passive aggression. Aggression, wherever it comes from, undermines the mutual trust needed for the preacher to communicate the Word and for the listener to hear it at the deepest level. It undermines the preacher personally because it puts him on a defensive footing. This in turn severs the delicate three-way connection between preacher and people, and what God's Spirit is communicating to them together. Both preacher and listeners must be open to the Word, waiting on it in a kind of vulnerability to each other which is often felt as a restrained and loving courtesy as they share the peace. Sharing the peace is a way of expressing gratitude and recognition for the gifts which others bring to the service of worship.

Knowing God's people

The preacher's vulnerability lies in a particular way of knowing God's people, the people he will be speaking to on Sunday morning. The call to love God's people is paramount in preaching, but it does not depend on knowing them personally. We must know and be vulnerable to our listeners even if we have never met them before. This means

---

7   Encouraging questions and active engagement with the sermon does not give listeners the right to heckle, as they did in the early years of non-conformism when '(the) frequent heckling of Quakers during Sunday services ... made the Quakers appear a serious threat to established authority'. See Susan Doran and Christopher Durston, *Princes, Pastors and People – The Church and Religion in England 1500-1689* (2nd edition), (London and New York: Routledge, 2003), p.133.

that preachers must bear those who will be listening to the sermon in the way he or she is called to bear the Word. The preacher must hold the people in a place of compassionate emptiness before God.

If the preacher knows them personally he may find that certain faces or personal situations come to mind, and he should try to visualise the face if possible, to 'listen' to the situation and love the person. He must also note his own feelings. Some of those in the congregation will be people who support and encourage him. He may find others intimidating, either because they appear to know more theology than he does, or because they resent or dislike him personally, or they are angry with some aspect of the institutional Church which he represents. The preacher, and anyone in public ministry, is also the recipient of grudge, resentment and plain fantasy. It is important to be able to tell the difference between all three of these states of mind and not to allow oneself to be overwhelmed by any of them, while at the same time retaining empathy and compassion for those concerned.

Preaching is not about us. This applies to all preaching contexts. The preacher may be inexperienced, perhaps on placement in an Oxbridge college or in a prominent city parish church. She may be intimidated by having to preach sermons to people who have taught her or who are senior figures in a university, or key members of a church. She may be afraid of upsetting her own peer group, who are perhaps in the congregation or serving alongside her, and some of whose theological views differ radically from hers. Dealing with fear in its various manifestations comes with the preaching commission. It is a reality which we must all face.

Fear comes in different shapes. There is the healthy fear of God which, when apprehended in the wrong way, becomes unhealthy as it melds with our personal insecurities causing us to doubt whether we are up to the task itself. There is also fear about practical things. Some of these fears will be addressed in more detail in later chapters. But my immediate concern is with the more existential fear we have about the validity, or truth, of what we are about to say, and hence of our own validity. It simply does not do to tell ourselves, even subconsciously, that if we try hard enough to believe what we are saying it will be true, either for us or for those listening to us. Belief, as I have already said, is not faith, and we are tasked with giving people something worthy of their faith.

So it is our faith which is being questioned, and we need to feel confident about our own faith as we prepare to preach to God's people. But confidence is not arrogance. As we step up to the lectern or pulpit we simultaneously drop to the depths of what we have known in a continuous and direct encounter with Christ during the past week and perhaps for most of our lives. The question being asked of us then is not 'do I really believe this?' but, as with Job, 'Do I really *know* it?' Have I known it in my 'beholding'[8] of God at all times and in all places? Have I known it in random moments, as when watching a gripping television serial my deeper attention is suddenly claimed by God? Have I understood it

---

8   See Chapter 4, note 17, p.72.

as an epiphany while thinking about this sermon, or about the life situation of someone I know or am close to? Have I encountered it in the face of the suffering stranger? Has it become my life's purpose? We surrender our lives to the people, as well as to God, when we preach, but we must do so with the authority which comes with theological competence.

Chapter 6

Engaging with Text

Blessed Lord, who caused all holy Scriptures to be written for our learning: help us so to hear them, to read, mark, learn and inwardly digest them that, through patience and the comfort of your holy word, we may embrace and for ever hold fast the hope of everlasting life, which you have given us in our Saviour Jesus Christ, who is alive and reigns with you and the Holy Spirit, one God, now and for ever.

Collect for Bible Sunday

We have listened to the readings, read in a rather lacklustre way. We have stood for the Gospel and we now wait to see if the preacher will engage us. We are momentarily curious. Does she have some urgent news for us, something which will transfigure the way we think about Scripture and about God in respect to our lives? What does she really want to say?

Herein lies the crux of the problem when it comes to preaching. What do we really want to say? We will only know what we want to say when we have waited deeply on God in the words of Scripture. So we need to be truthful to ourselves in regard to the Bible and aware that Scripture is, for many of our listeners, the touchstone of their faith. But while the Christian faith, and the faith journey of any one person, will be rooted in Scripture, it will also have been conditioned by that person's intellectual context and the extent to which they have allowed their intellect to be shaped by a sense of God's presence in their lives. How we think about Scripture, and how we communicate the Word, as we receive it from the readings set on any given Sunday, depends on this sense of God intimately present to the thinking process itself, to the extent that we allow that process to be governed by a particular kind of knowledge, the knowledge of the Spirit of the living God already 'at work' in it.[1]

In one of his last conversations with his disciples, Jesus tells them to 'abide' with him (John 15:4). The Greek word for 'abide' has much to tell us about the way we are to think about Scripture in relation to preaching. To abide means to settle in to a place, or with a person, rather than just stay the night. As I write this, I am looking at a small icon I have on my desk, below my computer screen. It is the icon of the *Pantocrator* in which Christ looks out at the viewer and invites our gaze to remain (or 'abide') with him. In one hand he points the viewer to himself and with the other he holds an open book inscribed with Greek or Slavonic words from Scripture. It is not the meaning of the words which is important, but the intent or purpose of the icon in relation to the viewer, and what, when taken together, the book and the figure of Christ elicit in the viewer's heart. The icon painter has created a particular perspective in which the viewer's gaze remains fixed on the face of Christ while

---

1   The writer of the fourth Gospel understands the 'work' of Christ, in both healing and teaching contexts, to be a continuation of the creative work of the Father and to the primal act of Creation itself (John 5:17). The preacher is commissioned to take part in this work.

also 'taking in' the open book. To abide with Christ means to allow ourselves to be drawn into his gaze and to return it. The open book suggests that it also involves a certain kind of listening, in regard to text.

As preachers, we read text with a 'listening eye'. We read and we 'mark' what we sense the text is speaking to us in the readings set for the day. In marking textual detail, we begin to 'learn' the idea. Churches will vary in the way readings are selected, but whatever reading the preacher is tasked with interpreting, there will always be something about it which speaks into his heart in the way the iconic Christ is 'speaking' as he returns the viewer's gaze. It may be a single word, or some aspect of the scene being described. This is what we must mark as we continue to hold the gaze of Christ. This mutual gazing activity is the beginning of the learning process. The viewer may not initially be able to name the 'idea'. It will have to remain unnamed until God chooses to reveal it. But the preacher is always waiting on the idea, waiting on the word, waiting on the moment. She is waiting for whatever secret is at work in the text to be revealed to her. She waits for the secret in a state of alert but unhurried readiness, so that she can share it in an unhurried way with her listeners.

Waiting on this moment is the greatest of tests. It requires that we almost simultaneously remember and 'forget'. While we may initially remember or think of a particular idea with the rational part of our brain, we also note how these thoughts play into our on-going working relationship with God, whether or not they connect with it, and to what extent they either enhance or detract from it. We do this at the level of 'deep mind' where we know ourselves as God knows us. We might do the same in regard to someone for whom we sense that a given text will be particularly challenging or revelatory, entrusting them to God who knows them as he knows us.

In terms of our own thought process, we begin by paying attention to our feelings and remind ourselves of where they originate in our emotional landscape. Then we 'forget' them. We let them go. Our own feelings should not skew the interpretation of the text. They are there as a *point de repére*, a starting point for our thinking, even as we are preaching, but they should seldom be directly referred to. They must simply be accepted and then allowed to fade, so that wisdom can be revealed through them.

We learn by making sense of our lives through our contemplation of God in the reading of Scripture. This is how the preacher's own life experience is of great value to those listening. Aspects of her life will surface through the text, not only as memories, but as epiphanies or 'moments of truth'. The text, taken into her gazing on the abiding Christ, transfigures her understanding of memories. Ultimately, these experiences, and the understanding which they bring, will become part of the greater design which is God's purpose for the sermon. They will be woven into the wisdom of her words, almost without the preacher realising it. In allowing her memories to be re-formed through the text, the preacher is also broadening her own faith. She is making sense of what she believes in the light of truth and she takes the people with her as she speaks. The sermon should invite people to move from belief to faith. It should never manipulate or coerce. The preacher is not there to force people to read or interpret Scripture in the way she does. She is there to convey the purpose of the sermon. Its purpose is to enable an encounter to take place between Christ and his people, so that they can 'abide' with him in freedom.

Earlier, I said that faith takes us beyond belief. While belief in the 'logic' of God's existence, and in the actuality of the events recounted in the Gospel, informs our faith, simple belief will not sustain it indefinitely. What we believe must now be 'known' as a deeper truth. In the words of the philosopher Paul Ricoeur, 'Testimony about facts is linked to testimony about truth'.[2] What we believe still matters, and the historical truth of the events matters, which is what Paul meant when he wrote that if we do not believe in the Resurrection we are 'still in our sins'. It follows that the event of the Cross serves no purpose whatever if it is something we either choose to 'believe' or not. Its purpose lies in revealing who Jesus was and the meaning of the event for each one of us.

The question, therefore, is not 'Do I believe in God?' But do the texts of the day reveal God to me in a new way? Where do I encounter Christ? And from this, where will those who are listening to me encounter him? What 'idea', sourced in the tradition which I inhabit, and emerging from my deeper consciousness, will speak to my listeners and to the times we live in?[3]

If we have been gazing on, or contemplating, the face of Christ as the 'way in' to our sermon, our ideas will no longer be our own. They will be the fruit of his on-going work in us. They will be secrets revealed to us which pertain to the

2   Paul Ricoeur in Anna Carter Florence, *Preaching as Testimony*, p.63.
3   *Ibid.* p.2.

human heart and to the human condition in the world. These secrets also lie dormant in the hearts of our listeners, so the preacher's task in the preceding days will be to learn the secret which is operating beneath the surface of any given text, of the story told by, or about, any individual, including Jesus himself, so that the preacher can reveal the secret which is already in the hearts of her listeners.

Why this story? Why these events? These are the initial questions which challenge her. Here, the lectionary, or set of prescribed readings, can be helpful. They point the preacher in a particular direction. They invite her to follow the scarlet thread, a particular line of colour which gives a shape to the readings, even if that thread is barely discernible. It is very often in the Old Testament that we first catch sight of it.

Preaching on the Old Testament

Preachers tend to avoid the Old Testament. We are afraid that it might make us sound irrelevant or boring, or that we lack the scholarly competence needed to lend authority to what we say. As a result of these inhibitions, many preachers will either remain in the shallows with regard to this part of the Bible, and this is what can make them sound boring or irrelevant, or simply avoid it altogether. The solution to our lack of confidence lies in paying attention to commentaries and competent Old Testament study. Preachers need a certain amount of grounding in the basics of biblical studies and in the theology of the Bible if what we say about the Old Testament is to carry any weight, but this does not mean that the preacher must be a biblical scholar in order to bring to light the hidden treasures that lie between its pages. Prayerful thought and reading will yield surprising results.

The preacher must be prepared to be surprised by the Old Testament if he is to surprise and engage his listeners. He must also know that while his authority as a preacher comes from his learning, this does not give him permission to simply parade knowledge. The more he knows, the more he should respect the limitations of his intellectual knowledge. While the preacher needs to have grasped at least some of the facts and background to a text, so that the scarlet thread of truth which runs through the reading can connect with the truth already lodged in the heart of the listeners, and of the preacher himself, these facts are only the jumping off point for a deeper searching.

Here is an example of what I mean. I have chosen the passage (Isaiah 38:9-20 REB) at random. It happens to be one of a number of possible readings set for the Third Sunday of Easter. The passage could be described as the overview of a life-determining event, in this case the near fatal illness of King Hezekiah. It is told as a short ballad. The words which stayed with me come in the final verse 'the Lord is at hand to save me; so let the music of our praises resound all our life long in the house of the Lord'. Although I have not yet read the other texts set for the day, I am alert to the sense of hope, joy and gratitude expressed in these lines. But I also know that they express Hezekiah's reluctance to face political realities, notably the imminent invasion of King Sennacharib's forces and the inevitable deportation of Hezekiah's people to Babylon which will follow. They contrast sharply with the rest of the passage, which is probably why I am drawn to them. They will remain with me for a while, perhaps for the rest of the week.

During that time I will recall that they are spoken in the first person. It is 'I' and 'we' who are saying them. So these are words which embrace both the speaker and those who are listening to him and worshipping with him. This commonality of purpose may well be a key factor leading to the underlying truth of the sermon as a whole. I may detect it again, as the scarlet thread of truth, in subsequent readings for that day. Until then, I remain with these words, while also allowing them to speak from their historical context, and to raise their own questions, so that I can learn something from them.

There are questions to be answered. Does this particular historical context suggest that 'quietism', a passive state of being in the presence of God often leading to a state of denial about political realities, is an adequate substitute for the struggle of prayer? The political realities which underpin the passage could be the jumping off point for an exploration of this question. Or are these words simply an affirmation of faith in God's saving power? At what point do these two ideas converge? Again, the preacher will be helped by knowing something of the historical circumstances pertaining to the passage.

While retaining a focus on these ideas, and on the questions they raise, the preacher must also hold God's people, who she will be speaking to on Sunday, in the presence of the living God. What will these words mean for them, in their particular circumstances, both personal and shared? What will it mean to know that 'the Lord is at hand to save me' and 'to let the music of our praises resound all our life long in the house of the Lord'? Do these words speak into our own fears about the troubled world of today?

This is where the preacher must take the words of such a text into the people's need for God. Some will not have fully acknowledged this need, but all are there, ostensibly at least, to praise him, and to do so 'all their life long in the house of the Lord', but the preacher risks becoming a hostage to fortune if she dwells too quickly, and possibly too clumsily, on the desirability of attending church on a Sunday. So she must sense another meaning, a deeper truth at work in this passage. What might the 'house of the Lord' signify outside the walls which she and the people are currently occupying? What does it mean to praise God for one's whole life? Somewhere she will pick up the thread, the secret at the heart of this ballad, which is that praise of God *is* life and that it goes on within us for as long as we return his gaze. Life in its fullest sense ceases, and the fear which gives birth to sin lodges itself in the human heart, from the moment we refuse to return God's gaze.

The Old Testament speaks of a people's relationship with God which, like all relationships, goes through periods of difficulty. There are times when God appears to have abandoned his people, or to be indifferent to their suffering, or to the suffering of any one individual; Job, for example, or the suffering servant in the book of Isaiah. This sense of abandonment by God, and the kind of dialogues which it produces, is one of the richest preaching resources in the Bible. Job is every man, woman and child who struggles with apparent contradictions in the purposes of God. The suffering servant is Christ alongside every victim of injustice, oppression and humiliation, great or small, inflicted by the envy of others.

For this reason, it is always worth taking the time and the interest, to keep abreast of current scholarship in regard to aspects of the Bible that particularly interest the preacher. Some of these will put familiar passages in an entirely new light and challenge our understanding not only about God, but about the origins of monotheistic worship in the Judaic tradition, for example.[4] This is an area which excites me personally and I refer to it, not because of its intrinsic importance, but in order to draw attention to the fact that the person preaching needs to have regular contact with those books of the Old Testament which particularly interest her, or to which she feels instinctively drawn.

Preaching on the Old Testament requires that we know *why* we want to talk about it, why its words sometimes baffle us, why we are at times even repelled by it and why we are also drawn to it. We can be certain that at least some of the people listening to us will have similar ambivalent feelings in regard to this part of the Bible, so we need to be in a position to offer them new and creative ways of thinking about the Bible as a whole, rather than simply providing them with ready-made answers or vague coping mechanisms for dealing with areas of the Old Testament that they find hard to understand or to accept.

---

4   Here, I would recommend Margaret Barker's work in which she argues for an understanding of Christianity, and especially of Christian liturgy, as proceeding from the earliest Temple tradition of Judaism, as it was instated by Solomon. See Margaret Barker, *Temple Theology: An Introduction* (London: SPCK, 2004).

Commentaries and more general books on aspects of the Old Testament should form part of every preacher's library. The information they give not only provides essential 'ballast' for the sermon itself, it also dispels some common theological misconceptions, so helping us to discern the truth of Scripture in which is lodged the 'idea' that God would have us share with his people. Well-informed sermons make for confident preaching.

Michael Thompson, Vice Principal of Ridley Hall, the theological college where I trained, would often remind us that 'If there's a mist in the pulpit, there's a fog in the pews'. Knowing a little about historical context, literary source and any possible editorial 'slant' in relation to the Old Testament helps to dispel the general mist of ignorance and inherited misunderstanding in which the preacher sometimes shares. One such misconception is that the Old Testament is primarily about the coming of Christ so that anything else is, at best, only of passing interest. This can give rise to the notion, seldom acknowledged, that the gospel is the only reading which really 'counts'. Such an approach constrains the preacher, both theologically and spiritually. It leads to a partial understanding, and hence a distortion, of the underlying idea which runs through all the set readings, and makes them cohere. A partial understanding of the readings set for the day blocks the on-going life of God's word, which is the activity of the Holy Spirit speaking through the texts as a whole. So the preacher will need to keep her eyes on the 'horizon', on the broader picture as it is afforded by all the texts, looking for the thread which connects them and pondering its implications for the people she is speaking to.

Preaching on the gospels

The gospel set for the Third Sunday of Easter, alongside the Isaiah reading above, tells the story of the raising of Lazarus (John 11: 17-44).[5] The preacher, as well as many of the people listening to him, will know it well. But the preacher needs to read it again, almost as if for the first time, not only during the preceding week, but as he reads it aloud to the people on Sunday. He must allow it to do its work on *him*, or it will not do its work on the people. It will only do its work if, during the preceding days, it has become part of the preacher's inner being, part of his breathing, and his own place of 'returning', even when he was not consciously thinking of it. Only when he is present to the gospel in this way will the preacher grasp the thread, the underlying idea and its particular significance for the moment.

During the week, the preacher will allow the story of the raising of Lazarus to transfigure his understanding of faith and of his own mortality.[6] This may be the thread which ties the gospel to the Old Testament reading. He must be prepared for surprises, for something unexpected to emerge from the text as a kind of 'epiphany'. He may be surprised, for example, by his own reaction to the words of Martha, Mary's sister, 'Lord, if you had been here, my brother would not have died'. Does he share her anger? Or perhaps her momentary lapse of faith? Or is this in fact a *sign* of her faith? Does he identify with Christ's anger in the face of

---

5   Church in Wales lectionary 2015/2016.
6   The preacher also needs to be aware that this story may have a profound effect on anyone in the congregation who is nearing the end of their life or who may have been recently bereaved.

our human mortality? Is the preacher himself angry about the death of someone he loves? These are some of the questions he will need to ask himself if he is to know *why* he is preaching on this text, what drives his thinking. He will also need to think deeply about the prayer of Jesus to the Father and the idea of this miracle being wrought for the sake of the people watching (v.42). What does Jesus want to teach them about the life which comes from God? And how does this relate to 'life' as it is described in the Isaiah reading?

To inhabit a gospel event in this way is to 'inwardly digest' its meaning, as the Collect for Bible Sunday says. Something similar happens in the context of parables and stories that have a metaphorical sub-text as, for example, the story of the feeding of the five thousand. Where it is given as a set text for a particular Sunday, it will usually be accompanied by the story of the miraculous 'manna' from heaven which fell on the heads of the hungry Israelites as they wandered in the wilderness (Exodus 16). Both stories invite reflection on the meaning of faith in God, and on what kind of God we say we believe in, as well as on the meaning and purpose of prayer itself. The extent to which prayer brings us close to God, and makes us vulnerable to his grace, will depend on how we view God in the first place.

Parables are metaphors about God and about our relationship with him. At times, the imagery can seem arcane, or the message completely at odds with post-modern western ethics and social mores, but a world and mentality different from our own does not make for irrelevance. It requires that we 'reconfigure' how we see things. We retain the emphasis but change the focus.

Take the parable of the talents, for example (Matt.25:14-30). The talent was a weight, or currency, used by the Romans and Greeks. The story can be read in a number of ways and begs a number of questions. Is it an endorsement of free market capitalism? If so, is it perhaps telling us that profit must lead to liberality and generosity towards others as well as self, and of the consequences of timid selfishness? Or is it about another kind of talent, our natural gifts and our uniqueness as persons in the eyes of God? If this is so, our natural gifts must also be employed for the greater good, in love for God, rather than because we are afraid of failure. If we deny our own giftedness, or allow others to deny it to us, our humanity withers and dies. The talents parable might draw us into thinking about the disappointments many people feel when they reach mid-life or old age. Oscar Wilde once said that at the moment of death, we shall only regret the things we never did. We shall only regret having buried our 'talent'. So the parable of the talents is also a cautionary tale about the dangers of wasting one's life because we are afraid of what people (those who we secretly envy or whose *persona* we covet and would like to emulate) would think if we did what we really want to do, so defying them, by confronting our own demons in becoming the person we really are. The parable of the talents could be about the courage it takes to be truly free.

Here, it is also worth noting what Paul says about counting all material gain, including that of status and power, as loss compared to the profound joy of knowing Jesus Christ. (Phil. 3:8) He is not condemning the world, or belittling the respect given to the wise and the learned. Neither is he denying our need for the basics of life. He is urging his listeners to pay attention to the needs of the human spirit, the human need for God, which is supremely met in Jesus Christ.

What is most important about parables is the manner in which they awaken or feed people's hunger for a deeper knowledge of God. How we think about God may well decide what we do, or fail to do, with our lives. If we have turned God into an angry idol, a 'Zeus' figure, we will spend our lives conforming to what we think are the idol's expectations.[7] The 'Zeus god' stands over and against the God who is, of his own nature, *for* human beings, a subtle but significant truth at work in the parable of the talents. Seeing the master in the story as an angry unappeasable God skews the story. The parable now becomes all about the individual's failure to please and placate, and his failure to 'achieve' salvation through his own efforts. But if the master's anger relates to the servant's unwillingness to trust in the grace given to him (the 'talent') to become fully the person he was created to be, we see the effect of our own obstinate refusal to work with the passionate love of the Father in some of the choices and decisions we make, or fail to make, in our lives. The truth of the parable lies in the man's wanting to remain in a state of infantile dependency which is sustained by inappropriate or unrealistic expectations of the person 'in charge'. In the life of the Church, or of a particular worshipping community, those expectations can be reinforced by power-infatuated individuals and helped by religious conditioning which fosters negative emotions of guilt and fear. This kind of dominant-

---

7   See Maggie Ross, *Pillars of Flame*, Chapter 3, 'Ways of thinking about God: Can Athens and Jerusalem ever meet?', p.59 ff.

subservient relationship, and the emotions it elicits, does not constitute mature Christian faith.

Preaching on the Pauline epistles

The Pauline epistles frequently return us to the importance of mature faith. Paul's concern for his churches is that people should move from one way of being in relation to God, the way of the Law, to another, the way of freedom in Christ. This is the 'idea', the scarlet thread of truth, which runs through much of his writing and ties it together. It gives it the kind of unity which Paul desires for individual churches and for the Church as a whole. Take, for example, the passage from Romans (Rom. 8:31-39). I have chosen this passage from Romans on the basis that the letter is generally thought to summarise all of Paul's work: In Christ we are free. When preaching on Paul, and not only on Romans, the preacher will need to hold this idea of freedom in Christ at the forefront of her thinking. Even when the text dwells on other matters, Paul will invariably return the reader to Christ and to the universal nature of his authority and saving grace. Christ is the incarnation of the God who is *for* humanity.

As the preacher begins to look at the Romans text, she will need to know this truth, as it is explicitly stated in v.31, at the deepest level of her own consciousness, in that place where she holds in secret the meaning and purpose of her own life. The truth, and the meaning and purpose of her life, whatever it has been, will invariably return her to Paul's words, 'If God is for us, who is against us?' She will therefore need to be true to herself in the way she thinks about these words. Depending on whether she is going through a crisis, or at a time when life is particularly rich and good, the words will speak differently to her. This does not mean that she must personalise her sermon on the basis of how she is feeling at the moment, but her own self-awareness will authenticate whatever she is given to say, so that her listeners will recognise the truth of her words whatever their current circumstances.

Much of Paul's writing pertains to what is called the 'eschaton', the 'last times', or what we might call the 'in between times'[8]. They pertain on one level to the period we all live in, which is the time of waiting for Christ to appear in glory. They also pertain to our separate lives in the present, lives lived in the hope, or the refusal, of God's blessing of grace. Grace is given to us so that we can respond to God's invitation to be 'at one' with him in Christ, which is the true meaning of atonement.[9] Earlier, I said that the preacher's task lies in understanding the people we are speaking to in and through Christ.[10] The preacher must not get in the way of this work. The Romans text, as well as Paul's letter to the Philippians, are well suited to such an exercise. They speak of God's self-emptying, his kenotic generosity, in the giving of his Son who is the 'way' itself, as well as the truth and life. God's 'not withholding' of his Son is the ultimate act of generosity to the human race.

The sermon might invite listeners to consider how we react to such generosity and to the generosity of other people. Do we sometimes find it hard to receive because

---

8   See Chapter 4, p.69, note 11.
9   See my *Making Sense of God's Love: Atonement and Redemption*.
10   See Chapter 3.

we feel unworthy in some way? For many of us, perhaps, life has been mistaken for a race to acquire sufficient merit to allow us not to have to feel indebted to anyone. Being in debt can make us feel exposed and vulnerable. But, says Paul, 'Who will bring any *charge* against God's elect?' With these words our timid efforts to respond to God's grace are owned in Christ's vulnerability. We become vulnerable in his risen body as it is so beautifully portrayed in the Bernini painting, *Christ Blessing*.

Our efforts as preachers are graced by Christ's working in and through us, so that we can be a blessing to others. It is not we who preach the word of God, but God who imparts life through what we are to his people, and thereby through what we say.

Chapter 7

Times and seasons

In his book *The Wounded Healer* Henri Nouwen describes a hospital visit. A man is about to have a life determining operation, from which he does not ultimately recover. He is being visited by a young curate. The curate follows standard counselling procedure which amounts to asking questions and repeating the person's reply. It is more of an interrogation process than a conversation. The man is afraid that he may die. He wants his life back, and the full use of his legs. But the one-sided conversation does not give him permission to talk about his fear of dying. The curate has been unable to meet him in it, to offer him the hospitality of the presence of Christ in which they both share in this particular moment.

This is the hospitality which the preacher must offer to his listeners, the hospitality of an encounter with another person, which takes place in Christ in the grief or joy of the moment. For such an encounter to be possible he must love his listeners, even if he has never met them. He must love them as God's people and be fully present to them. The best teachers, and the best preachers, are those who love the people they teach.

Preaching is both a teaching and a pastoral ministry. The pastoral task is also sacrificial. It involves meeting people in Christ, not by expecting them to defer to our perceived clerical authority, or to our particular spiritual or denominational theology. We have to be prepared to die to all these things, beginning with the outer trappings of status and authority, so that others can encounter Christ in us in their time of need. It is more important that they encounter Christ than that they come to think as we do on any given issue. They must encounter him in and through the Christ-like persons we are. This is where real authority lies.

The pastoral nature of preaching means that there are practical implications for breaking down the denominational walls which so often separate us from the people. Within the Anglican tradition, an evangelical cannot assume that he will always be taking the funeral of another evangelical. Neither will it do for an Anglo-Catholic to refuse to accommodate himself to the liturgical and dress norms of the evangelical family to whom he is called to minister in their time of grief. As preachers, we must therefore be prepared to shed our identity, and even our reputation, in these areas. The evangelical preacher must risk disappointing her denominational peer group in order to speak the liturgical language of those whose theology she may not agree with.

To speak someone's language is to get into another's thought process and embrace it, and so understand what makes them 'tick'. This is what happens when a person grows up speaking more than one language fluently. If you speak French or Spanish, you become French or Spanish to the person you are speaking to. Where there is grief the preacher is called to become the person who is grieving, not with demonstrative tears and ineffectual talk, but with 'sighs too deep for words', and with silence. Out of this graced silence come the compassion, wisdom and confidence which the person who is preaching or presiding at a funeral will need.

Preaching at funerals

If she is preaching at a funeral she will have been helped by earlier meetings with the family and possibly by her own personal knowledge of the one who has died. Irrespective of the text, her task will be to bring the goodness of that particular life into focus so that others can rejoice in it. To rejoice in another's life in the midst of grief is to live the resurrection. It marks the beginning of eternal life. All who are present, including the person leading the service, share, and are kin, in this eternal life. As a result of the trust placed in her by the family when she visited them and offered them Christ's hospitality in their grief, a kinship will have been established between her and them and between her and the people attending the funeral. It corresponds to the kinship which Jesus felt with the woman who was on her way to her son's funeral, (Luke 7:11-17) with the family of the little girl whom he raised from a coma, (Mark 5:41) and with the Roman centurion whose loved servant he also brought back to life (Luke 7:2-10).

Preachers are called to speak life and hope into death and despair. Jesus promised that those who keep faith with him would not see death, although they would have to pass through the gate of mortality before entering eternal life. The mourners need to hear this and know it for themselves. The preacher must know it too. Only then will he be able to convey the idea of eternal life as a deeper kind of living, a living in and from the love of God, beginning in the present moment. It is in this present moment, as the mourners are gathered in the church or crematorium chapel, that we know something of what the eternal life promised by Jesus is about. It is about enduring love. The love of God is the inexhaustible source of grace and peace which sustains us in our grief and will continue to sustain us in the days and weeks to come, if we allow it. Eternal life pertains to the 'now and the not yet'. It is outside linear or historical time as we know it. It is a time and a dimension in which we continually encounter the living God.

Handling emotion

The preacher must bring all of her life to the preaching task, so that she can effect this encounter with the love of God in the present moment, by offering the mourners the hospitality of Christ through her preaching and in her presence to their grief. This being said, there will also be times when she finds that some aspect of her personal life, or of parish relationships which impact on her directly, puts her feelings completely at odds with theirs and with the event into which she is ministering. The same is true of liturgical seasons. In both cases she is susceptible to the emotions around her, as well as to her own.

The preacher must face her own feelings and work with them if she is to encounter her listeners in theirs and make it possible for them to own and share them in Christ. This does not mean that she should suppress her emotions, but she does need to be in a state of emotional equilibrium. She must not allow her feelings to swamp the sermon, or destabilise the service. While vulnerability is important, those who are tasked with leading public worship in the context of life transitioning events should avoid embarrassing their listeners. The same is true in the context of charismatic worship. If the preacher is too visibly carried away by his emotions, he will lose touch with the people and lose sight of the direction of the service.

Nevertheless, there are times when it is hard for the person preaching to 'hold' the people's emotions and at the same time bring a degree of gravitas and detachment to the service, especially to a funeral. Loving detachment is essential in this context. If the minister or preacher is a close friend or relative of the deceased, he will inevitably be one of the mourners, and even if the minister does not know the person, he will have been drawn into the family's grief in helping them prepare for the funeral. In the latter case, his relationship with that family will be both transient and intimate and this also can be emotionally challenging. His task is therefore not only to mourn with those who mourn, and to take their grief to God at a time when they may not have the emotional resources for doing this, but to allow his own feelings to be identified with theirs whether or not he knows the family well. Loving detachment and emotional equilibrium are essential in both cases.

Equilibrium and detachment come with stability in our life in God. Together, they constitute what Maggie Ross describes as 'equipoise', a state of 'moving balance and repose' in God which takes us beyond our limited selves.[1] If the preacher's emotional life in God has rhythm and depth, she will have taken time to find her equipoise, and to centre herself on the task in hand before the service begins. This will involve, first of all, owning her own grief alongside the family's and allowing that ownership to be effected at the deepest level. If she knows the family or the deceased personally, she will need to have done her own weeping. This is what Jesus did outside the tomb of Lazarus. He wept for himself. He then took his friends' grief into his own, and into the re-creative anger heard in his command to Lazarus to come out of the tomb. If we have not fully owned our grief, if we have not wept as Jesus did, we will not be able to offer his hospitality to those listening to us. The same is true even if we do not know the person who has died, because the family's grief becomes ours too. But if we let our emotions take us by surprise, which can happen even when we do not know the person, we will not be in a position to take their grief to Christ. We will be too anxious about maintaining a grip on our own suppressed emotions. So we must first weep, if we need to, and then entrust our emotions to God who will hold them for us until we have completed our task.

But what happens when the opposite is true? We may be about to preach at a funeral having just received wonderful news about someone we love, or been confirmed in a decision relating to our own lives. We are jubilant. Must we then fake grief? Of course not. What is required is simple gratitude for whatever is making us happy in the moment, owned and then

---

1   Maggie Ross, *Pillars of Flame*, p.85.

entrusted to God. The emotional 'processing' is the same. We entrust our joy and gratitude for whatever is happening in our lives to our heavenly Father, as Jesus would have done on numerous occasions when he ministered to the suffering and those who mourned. We focus on the emotional needs of the people we are serving at this moment. This is not faking. It is simply a different kind of sacrifice, the setting aside of our own happiness in order to enter into the grief of others, so bringing them the hospitality of Christ.

Seasonal variations

All that I have said so far also applies to our feelings in relation to the liturgical seasons. Christmas can prove to be one of the most demanding times for clergy and for those who preach, as it is for many people. It is full of paradox and contradictions. It may coincide with the anniversary of someone's death or it may prove to be the final cause of relationship breakdown.[2] There will be those who are deeply anxious about debt, but do not want to spoil things for their children, or perhaps for their partner, by sharing this anxiety. Global conflict and terrorism also foment anxiety, as do extreme weather conditions at home. The preacher may be experiencing difficulties in his own life. Taken together, these contemporary life situations, along with the crass materialism

---

2   According to the UK Family Mediation helpline, 1.8 million people contemplate divorce during the Christmas period, and Relate, a leading UK relationship support charity, has been known to receive a 50 per cent increase in calls at this time. (Data source metro.co.uk October, 2009.) But more recent figures indicate that Christmas itself is not necessarily the cause of the breakup. ('January divorce day? Christmas off the hook' *The Telegraph*, 21 April, 2016).

which is often the root cause of unseasonal depression at Christmas, make the season feel unreal and disconnected from the hard realities of living in the world.

With all of these negative feelings comes a sense of guilt. We feel we have failed because our own emotions do not match the season. But feeling unhappy at Christmas is not a sin. We are not disappointing God by feeling depressed as we lead a carol service. In fact, trying to be happy when one has every reason not to be makes a nonsense of Christian joy. Guilt is entirely counter-productive. Christian joy was bought with suffering, so it helps to remember that the seasonal joy of Christmas and Easter comes at some cost to the One who made them possible in the first place. The cold and inhospitable circumstances surrounding the birth of Christ did not have much sparkle about them. He came into the hard core reality of the world as it is, and that includes where we happen to find ourselves on life's journey on Christmas Day.

There is a particular kinship at work at this time, irrespective of prevailing emotions. The Incarnation reminds us of God's hospitality towards human beings in his embracing of the human condition. The preacher knows that her own circumstances or state of mind, as well as the lives of those she is preaching to, are part of the human condition; that we are together in something which is not simply about us, or even about our particular church or worshipping community. We are held together in Christ in all our emotions and life experience, whether or not they fit with the season. Christmas is an encounter with God which encompasses both grief and joy. In all these things we are claimed by God in our lives as they are now.

The same is true, in a different way, of Easter. Here, we are challenged by the enormous emotional turnaround which must be effected between Good Friday and Easter Sunday. The Sabbath provided by Holy Saturday is a gift for the preacher. It affords her time to take stock of recent events so that she can reflect on them in the context of the bigger picture. The Saturday space allows us to think of the world in the light of how all things will be when Christ comes again, but to think of them as if they were happening now. We live in a Good Friday world, but we also live in the realised expectation of Easter. It is an 'already but not yet' time.

I have long felt that Holy Saturday is better suited for 'end time' reflection than the Sundays preceding Advent. There is a sense of Christ's absence about it which invites us to think about how he will 'come again in glory to judge the living and the dead', as the Christian creed puts it. This sense of absence is important. It gives us time to bring the suffering and dying of Christ into the light of his rising again and, in so doing, try to make sense of the world and of our lives through the prism of these events. Irrespective of the texts set for Easter Sunday, the preacher will need to have spent time in this particular conceptual space. It is traditionally thought of as the time of Christ's descent into hell. Even if the preacher has already spoken of Christ's dereliction on the Cross on Good Friday, she may find it helpful to return to the picture of that same Christ descending into hell on Holy Saturday.

Holy Saturday is the great prelude to Easter. It is when Christ rescues Adam and all those who have died before ever having met Jesus Christ in their lives. Icon painters sometimes depict the descent into hell as a rending of the earth into which Christ descends to drag up Adam as though from the ruins of an earthquake. I think that he drags despairing Judas out of the rubble too, along with all those who have given up on themselves and on the possibility of a merciful and loving God seeking them out in their own particular hell, so that he can embrace them into his risen life. These ideas will profoundly affect how the Resurrection is conveyed to those who may only come to church at Easter or for the funerals and weddings of family and friends. The Resurrection of Christ is an open secret. It is something which the most entrenched agnostic cannot quite let go of, and whose significance even the most committed Christian has barely begun to grasp. It takes us beyond ourselves into a different way of thinking about the meaning and purpose of human existence and of life itself in all its manifestations.

Preaching at weddings

Weddings celebrate life and it is the preacher's task to speak of the fullness of that life in the way Jesus meant it to be understood. One of the most popular readings at weddings is the story of the marriage feast at Cana in Galilee when Jesus saves a couple and their parents from the embarrassment of running out of wine at the reception (John 2:1-11). The new life promised us in Jesus begins with our being saved from embarrassment. The death and Resurrection of Jesus is about God's sharing of a shameful secret (what we call sin) which he then effaces. The sharing takes place on the Cross and the effacing happens in the hearing of our name being called by the risen Christ. In the case of the marriage feast at Cana the shameful secret was that the couple could not afford the hospitality expected of them and its effacing was the transformation of water into wine of the highest quality.

While the preacher may not want to dwell on the subject of sin and shame in the context of a marriage service he should have known what it is to experience failure and embarrassment in his own life if he is to convey the deep joy of the Resurrection to his listeners. This joy informs the marriage vows and will sustain the couple in the years to come. But the preacher treads a fine line. He must be sensitive to those who otherwise rarely come to church but he must also surprise them, without embarrassing them or the couple. For this to be possible he needs to be deeply grounded in his own 'knowing' of God which, as I said in an earlier chapter, is entirely mutual. We know and are known by a God who wishes us joy. The wedding sermon will invite listeners to remember the joy of this particular moment. It pertains to God and it sources and sustains trust. The preacher will encourage the two people who are about to make vows to each other to make a habit of 'returning' to it in their life together, as they promise to be faithful to one another 'for better or for worse'.

The brief exchange which takes place between Jesus, his mother and the master of ceremonies is a key element in conveying the idea of the reciprocated love and trust which exists between God and human beings. His mother knows her son, and she trusts him, so she can confidently override his objections to performing such a miracle ahead of his time. She tells the man in charge to simply do whatever Jesus tells him. Jesus does as he is bidden, not because his mother tells him to, but because of the potential dishonour for the couple should the wine run out. The miracle is a foretaste of salvation, a life-giving moment, a saving of the day. A secret has been shared and then effaced by love, so that the master of ceremonies can only be pleasantly surprised by the fact that the best has been kept until last.

If he is preaching on this text the preacher may also want to dwell on the deepening of love which will mature over the years into profound understanding between the two people being married. Each will 'know' what the other needs and will deploy all that they have to give, so that the other can be happy. This miracle is about celebrating the love of God, a love which knows no bounds when it comes to giving human beings what they most yearn for, even when they are not aware of that yearning.

1 Corinthians 13 and 1 John 4:7-12 are also frequently in demand at weddings. Both readings are about love. The language and cadence of these texts allows the preacher to introduce an element of gravitas into a sermon which might otherwise sound superficial or flippant, especially if he feels obliged to make his address sound light hearted and not too 'religious'. These two texts invite the preacher to step bravely away from the banal and allow the texts to speak through him so that the couple and those who are listening will have something enduring to take home with them, the love of God, for which they are also yearning.

The preacher might want to focus on the idea that it is God's own love for us which makes love between two people possible. As Maggie Ross writes, *'Only love can recognise Love. It is only because we bear, each one of us, each fragment of creation, the trace of the divine that we dimly recognise that the hunger crying out from every human heart can be fed by this radiance alone.*[3] The wedding sermon is for all who are present. It will create a bond of its own between the newly married couple and the friends and family who are witnessing the marriage, so it must be spoken *through* the couple to the people. It is not a private address to the couple. The people in the pews will also need to hear that they are loved by God and that they have love to give to others. Some of them may not have heard love spoken of in this way in the context of a church service. Setting the wedding homily within the greater framework of God's love for all the people present also creates a much needed emotional space for the couple. It diverts everyone's attention from them for a few minutes which in turn helps to make them feel less anxious and exposed as they prepare to exchange their vows.

If the person who is preaching is also conducting the marriage ceremony, she will have rehearsed the exchange of vows and rings with the bride and groom the evening before. It will help the couple, as well as her preaching, if during the rehearsal she emphasises the fact that this exchange of vows takes place between the two of them. They are not making their vows to the minister, or to their friends. They should face each other during the exchange and speak the words to each other, while remaining audible to their guests who are witnesses to this marriage. The sermon will help them to do this if it has emphasised the shared nature of the event. As with the vows, anything relating to the couple is best

---

3   Maggie Ross, *Writing the Icon of the Heart*, p.17.

said towards the end of the homily, directly to them, while remaining audible to the congregation.

Handling the unexpected

Weddings are as prone to the unexpected as any other service. With a little experience, the preacher will take interruptions and distractions, as well as unforeseen events in his stride. A colleague of mine once arrived just ahead of the bride having accidentally taken his wife's cassock. It was summer. He was wearing sandals and shorts, having just come from mowing the lawn, and the cassock reached just below his knees. He found another cassock in the vestry. Otherwise, he would have had to run home and get his own, generating as little anxiety as possible, for himself as well as everyone else.

Distractions and interruptions are not obstacles needing to be overcome. We need to take them in our stride. Where the preacher feels that she is 'up against' something, the people sense her tension and this creates a climate of anxiety in the pews. We do not help our listeners by making them anxious about us. Anxiety is not conducive to hearing the word of God, or to speaking it in a way which shapes meaning in the hearts and minds of both listener and speaker, so our personal anxiety has to be managed before we reach the pulpit. The preacher will undoubtedly have plenty of things on her mind but she cannot come to the task of preaching, and expect people to meet Jesus in what she says, if she brings these anxieties with her. She needs to be fully present to the people. She can only be present to them when she has been fully present to God for a reasonable period of time before the service, bringing the people to God during that time. They will only meet Jesus when they sense his love for them in the undivided attention they receive from the person who is preaching and ministering to them on Sunday morning. Furthermore, the preacher's love for the people will in itself transform interruptions and distractions into God's loving purpose for preacher and people alike. His purpose is always one of deep joy.

Jesus was never one for solemn religion. Joy and laughter enrich worship, so when it comes to interruptions and unexpected situations, the preacher should remember that all things work to the good for those who love God. Take, for example, what can happen when a family with two or three young children turn up unexpectedly for a service in a small and sparsely attended country church. The family may be passing through the area, or they may be occasional visitors. This is not a church which has regular family services. In fact few families with children ever come to it. Furthermore, the preacher's sermon does not particularly lend itself to young listeners, so he is anxious when he sees them step through the door, but he must allow his anxiety to be held in Christ, remembering that he himself is known and loved by God at this precise moment. So he should be confident in this love and approach the children without overwhelming them. If there is a children's corner, he should not be afraid to make use of it. It is not forbidden territory. He could make a point of going there to greet the children personally and speak with them before the service begins, even if this delays the start of the service by a few minutes. The word that he is waiting on may well sound clearly through these children, as I have found on a number of occasions in country churches.

When it comes to the sermon, irrespective of where the preacher is positioned, whether in the pulpit or at 'ground level', he needs to 'signal' to the children that he is there for them and not only for the adults. He might tell them that in a little while he is going to be talking to the grownups and perhaps give the children a small project to work on if facilities permit. The project should relate to the key element of his sermon. It could be a drawing, or a prepared thought or prayer. At the end of the sermon, or at the end of the service if he prefers, he invites the children to come forward and share what they have done. Wisdom and trust in the loving kindness of God will speak through these children because their angels continually behold his face. Children are always in conversation with God. There will be joy and laughter when they produce their prayers and drawings.

If we are always in conversation with God, if we continually return to him, and seek his abiding presence at all times and in all places, we shall know his faithfulness. God's faithfulness encompasses our anxieties. His abiding Spirit will be present to us in the moment that we begin speaking. It is a matter of equilibrium and detachment, of 'equipoise', of waiting on the word in this 'liminal' place. Maggie Ross writes that *'[Liminality] is the threshold where effects of unseen communication with, and input from, the deep mind become manifest. The person must wait in liminality, in unknowing, for gratuity, for whatever irrupts – often unawares – from the deep mind*[4] . In being rooted in Christ, as we wait in this liminal place, we are made fully available to his people when we speak. But we do not

4   Maggie Ross, *Silence*, p.47.

wait in a passive way. We must also ask for what we need. We must ask for the gift and wait for it in confident expectation that it will be given to us in the moment.

We must also ask that the people be given to us. This is not a request for power or control. We do not want to impress or influence them. We ask for them to be given to us because we love them. How we speak to the people, and not only what we say, will convey our love for them and so bring them to a deeper knowledge of God. Loving the people means sensing the concerns and questions which inhabit their minds and hearts on this particular Sunday morning. It is about knowing them in a particular way. We know them because we have held them in our own heart-thinking place throughout the week. Only when we know them in this particularly intimate way will we begin to sense what God wishes to say to them, and to us.

Chapter 8

Becoming a confident preacher

Brinkmanship, as defined by the Oxford Dictionary, is 'the art or practice of pursuing a dangerous policy to the limits before stopping'. It is also the art of sermon preparation. Good art is seldom produced by slavish adherence to unquestioned method. It is almost always produced by breaking rules in order better to keep them. The same applies to the art of preaching. We respect the boundaries of whatever method suits us best, including how and when we do the preparatory work which will underpin or validate the central tenet of the sermon, and we then forget about them. We break rules in order to realise their purpose. My purpose in writing this book has not been to give rules or define methods for preaching sermons. Whatever has been learned by way of technique and method is a tool for the trade but it is not preaching *per se*. As children, we are taught how to eat with a knife and fork, not to speak while chewing and, possibly, to refrain from using phones or laptops during family meals. There will be times when it will be fine to break any or all of these rules, but it is important to have learned them.

As a newly licensed lay reader, I was once advised by a senior cleric for whom I had great respect that if I wanted to preach without notes, or lead unscripted intercessions, I should do so straight away, or I would never do it. I did not entirely believe him and continued to write copious notes until the day came when, early on in the service, my notes fell under the chair I was sitting on. I was far too self-conscious to look for them, which left me with no choice but to preach 'blind'. There were only a handful of people in the church that Sunday, and a dog. The presence of the dog was reassuring as I had, until then, been in the habit of practising sermons from memory by speaking them to our two dogs. The dogs were an attentive, if excitable, little congregation but they were not people waiting on the Word of God. It was this consciousness of people waiting on God, and on his Word, which enabled me to preach that first sermon without notes. Unlike the dogs at home, the people were not waiting for me to just say something. They were waiting to hear something recognisable, a valid truth which would lead them into what T.S. Eliot called 'valid prayer'.[1] The purpose of preaching is to lead people to an inner place of their own where they will meet God in prayer.

The big idea

The truth of the sermon is valid to the extent that it has been shaped in the heart of the speaker as well as in his mind. This applies in whatever preaching context the speaker

---

1   A place 'where prayer has been valid', *The Four Quartets*, 'Little Gidding'.

finds himself, whether in a cathedral or church, a retirement home or children's service. The truth spoken from the preacher's place of encounter with God will resonate with something already known, or re-ignite a fire which already burns, even if unrecognised, in the heart of the listener. Sermon preparation is a way of intuiting that truth, gleaned from the texts during the week. So the preacher should wait, sensing the fire within, rather than worry and think about what he is going to say. We do not need to spend the week worrying about what we are going to say. Anxiety comes from allowing the creative process to be governed by the rational part of our thinking minds when we should be open to being surprised by what God may first have to say to *us*. Whatever we say to the people must be rooted in our own heart-thinking place, in the deep mind. The deep mind, or right side of the brain, is the place of 'not knowing' in which we know God and from which we are given the means to speak his Word.[2] While we may discover new things about the Bible and make new theological connections as we think and read, real surprise and genuine insight come from this different conceptual space. They are the result of our willingness to be *un*prepared and to take risks for the sake of that valid truth which our listeners need to hear.

Some of the best insights may come when the preacher is not engaged in formal sermon preparation. These are the vacant moments and distractions which are necessary to prayer. We waste time fighting them. Distractions can yield surprises and are to be brought to God along with everything

---

2   This is at the heart of Maggie Ross's thinking. For a visual representation of the functions of the left and right side of the brain see her chart in *Silence* pp.36-37.

else, in recognition that we are human and therefore not always in control of our thought processes. Being aware that we are not in control disposes us to be available to God. It disposes us to emptiness, a state of 'not knowing' which is essential to hearing the truth which God wishes to be spoken to his people on Sunday morning.

This is not to suggest that the person preaching should be like an empty bucket waiting for ideas to drop into it like pennies from heaven. We are not passive to the Word. Neither are we empty noisome vessels offering a few of our own pre-formed opinions, dressed up as reflections, which have been rattling around in our heads during the preceding week. We must bring silence to the preaching task by being open, conscious of our gift but deeply attentive to God. Our intellect is valuable, but it too is a gift, to be owned and then surrendered into that place in our deep mind where we know God without knowing what, if anything, we shall say about God. We wait on the Word. We wait in a state of expectancy which is about being reactive and, later perhaps, proactive, to and within the dynamic of God's Spirit. We wait in the 'not knowing'.

In the 'not knowing' of sermon preparation we are present to God, as he is to us. We can consciously remind ourselves of this by returning to a familiar mantra or short prayer, or to a word from the text itself, until it becomes almost part of our breathing Or, better still, we can simply acknowledge God's presence to us with love and gratitude in a continuous sub-liminal state of relatedness to God throughout the waking day, and on into the hours of sleep. This is what it means to pray constantly, to praise God 'at all times and in all places'. Love and gratitude are the heart's attentiveness to God. It is also this loving state of attentiveness to God which makes it possible for us to know when a distraction which we are in a hurry to dismiss is in fact the seed of the sermon, the seed which contains the big idea. God's Word already abiding with us interrupts the 'distraction', rather than the other way round, so making it possible for the ordinary and the everyday, for activities which do not, on the surface, seem to relate to prayer, to be the yeast which leavens the dough.

For example, those of us who get quite hooked on good television drama can find that a particular character or plot line stays with them for days, refusing to be ignored. Certain details will keep returning with pressing intensity. This is because there is truth in them. They resonate with something we already know, or with which we can identify because someone close to us has known it, or because it is part of a wider issue in society which we care about. If this 'distraction' persists, God may wish to use it. The big idea may be lodged somewhere within it. There may be connections to be made between the distraction and the texts set for the day which may not fully emerge until we are preaching.

Sensing connections with fiction, or with any external stimulus which shifts our inner focus away from ourselves and our immediate concerns, can be helpful to the preacher. Allowing our thoughts and feelings to 'run on' a little, into our distractions, conditions us to experience what it might feel like to be going through a particular trauma, or to be caught up in events which have a cathartic effect on people's lives but over which they may have no control. These intuitive feelings do not overwhelm us provided they are held within the matrix of constant prayer, of being in a continual state of beholding and listening to God.

The imaginative process depends on a continual sense of being in the presence of God. Thinking about what we are going to say is only part of the work of imagination. Thought and imagination are separate paths which ultimately lead to the same place, to an understanding which connects the preacher with her listeners so that, in the process of speaking and listening, both preacher and listener are connected with God.

Imagination has to be allowed, rather than worked at. Externals can echo the word already lodged in our 'not knowing', in our emptiness, but it is the Word itself which the preacher is listening for, as she sifts through the externals, or distractions, along with her attendant thoughts and feelings. This in turn is part of the not knowing process because it brings us up against ourselves, or against those things which get in the way of the work, the work of the dynamic and loving purpose of God's Spirit for his people. There is no method for arriving at this state of not knowing and of emptiness. It is gift. So we must ask for the gift with some urgency. Asking for the gift, and asking for the people to be given to us, is essential to the germination of the big idea. If we try to generate the idea solely with our own intellects, by working at it, we will end up with something which may not resonate with some of our listeners. It will sound 'worked up'. They are not waiting for a worked up sermon. They are waiting in a state of unknowing for the Word to meet them in their need for God.

Preaching as dialogue

This is the heart of the preaching paradox. As preachers, we wait in our emptiness and in our not knowing for the conversation which God wishes to have with his people. In our place of not knowing, we become the emissaries of the Word, the interpreters, the dialogue facilitators. We walk alongside Jesus on the road to Emmaus, and alongside his people. We read the texts *with* them as they are unfolded to us by the Spirit of the living God. The walk to Emmaus was a conversation. It was not a one-sided monologue. Jesus would have unfolded the Scriptures in such a way as to make it possible for the disciples to make the connections they needed in order to understand the true purpose of his coming, and of his being present to them in that moment. Having rebuked them for their dullness, possibly because they were asking all the wrong questions, he would have also loved them in their grief and confusion. He would have sensed the questions they really needed to ask. Something like this happens in preaching. The preacher senses the people's unspoken questions. The sermon is not a straightforward didactic process. It is a dialogue which takes place at the deepest level of our individual and collective consciousness. The survival of the Church depends on its ability to dialogue at this deep level, through its teaching ministry, with those on the fringes of its life.

New life generates growth, not just growth in numbers, but growth in love, love which comes from a deeply shared understanding of the truth as it is revealed in Jesus Christ. This is the love which overcomes fear. Fear separates people from one another and from the God we see in Jesus. For the Church, this separation leads to death. In the Church's life fear, and death, occur in a number of ways, all of which deal in untruthfulness, in Biblicism (or biblical idolatry), in ecclesial authoritarianism rooted in the imperialism of the first century,[3] in the ethics of exclusion and in the consumerism which drives the Church's missional life. God's presence is obscured in all these idolatries. The Church exists to liberate people from various forms of idolatry, so that they can have 'life in all its fullness' and the preacher is tasked with speaking this life into people's hearts.

Life emerges as a result of all parties involved in the teaching dialogue having understood the finality, or validity, of truth met in Jesus and focused into the Eucharist. The finality, the ultimate stopping point for life-destroying idolatry, is the Cross re-presented in the Eucharist. The preacher needs to be mindful of the Cross and of its all-embracing love, whatever the season. The truth, as understood through preaching, pertains to God's love for all human beings, so the preacher must also remain aware that truth is met in all the ways which women, men and children have of calling on the name of God, whatever their religion. The continuity of truth spans and embraces all of life, all that is. The Church is called to bear witness to the all-embracing love of God which we call truth. Shortly before he died, the theologian, Daniel

---

3   Christ's modelling of true authority did not sit well with the temporal power with which authority is often confused, to the extent that within decades of its conception Christianity was reduced to Christianism, a system, rather than a body, with authority modelled on that of the Emperor Tiberius. The organisational Church of today has retained this basic approach with its authority structures also shaped for the maintenance of the system. See Roger Haydon Mitchell, *The Fall of the Church* (Eugene, Oregon: Wipf & Stock, 2013), p. 32ff.

Hardy, in conversation with David Ford, is recorded as saying that thinking of Scripture and the Eucharist as part of a single and continuous encounter with God transforms the Church itself. The Church becomes 'a house of abundance'.[4]

The Church of the future will depend for its life and growth, and even for its continuing existence, on dialogue which leads to an understanding of the abundance of God's love for all people and for the on-going work of creation. The Church, and all people of faith, are called by God to take responsibility for this abundance. In the context of preaching, all participants are responsible for the work and for its outcome. The listener is responsible to the preacher in the way she listens, just as the preacher is responsible to the listener in the way he preaches. All must make connections as they journey together. This is what the disciples on the road to Emmaus initially failed to do. They were blinded by grief. They were living in a kind of limbo in which the prophecies foretold in the Old Testament no longer bore any obvious relation to Jesus, so that they failed initially to recognise him. They had encountered a break in the continuity of Scripture, a separation caused by their inability to trust in God and thus to 'hear' Jesus. They had not been able to wait sufficiently, or in the right way, for the reality of who Jesus was to become clear to them. The preaching dialogue prepares both listener and preacher for this same reality, the presence of the risen Christ among them made real in the sacramental word and in the Eucharist. But there is a danger that this could tie

4   Daniel W. Hardy with Deborah Hardy Ford, Peter Ochs and David F. Ford, *Wording a Radiance: Parting Conversations on God and the Church* (London: SCM, 2010), p.123.

the preaching task to the idea of sacrament, and this can alienate people for whom such language does not harmonise with their way of thinking about the Church and what its teaching and missional priorities should be. The preacher has to be theologically bi-lingual, or even multi-lingual, able to understand where others may be coming from, if she is to speak truthfully about a God who is for all.

Irrespective of his own churchmanship, the preacher is responsible for those whose theology and churchmanship differ from his own. He will need to dialogue with them, even if his sermon is taking him down paths which are strange to them. He must take responsibility for them by getting into their heart-thinking space, and asking their questions, when he thinks about his sermon during the preceding week. He must understand what shapes their theological language, so that he can better understand how to walk with them in the three-way dialogue for which he is responsible. He will not do this by patronising them with badly- expressed ideas borrowed for the occasion, or by ignoring them in the hope that they will somehow agree with him in the end. It is not his business to court popularity or strive anxiously for acceptance. Preaching and listening take us way beyond these limitations. Preaching obliges us to meet our listeners, especially those whose theology we do not necessarily share, before God, so we have to be prepared to love them in the ultimate place of encounter which is the Cross.

What shall I say? Preparing the sermon

There is a sense in which this is the totality of sermon preparation; meeting our listeners, whatever theological direction they are coming from, before God. We embrace them all before the Cross and wait on the Spirit of the living God to speak into our collective spiritual poverty. We therefore hope to preach what we ourselves need to hear, so that we can sense what God is really saying to this congregation today, not what we think we ought to say. Sermon preparation is about allowing the love of God to be revealed through our words. Whether we choose to write the words beforehand, or use bullet points, or simply speak what is given to us in the moment is not the most important consideration when it comes to sermon preparation. What is important is not getting in the way of the work itself, not obstructing the Word.

We prepare sermons by first attending to the needs of those we will be speaking to and to the needs of the world. Those ministering in a parish context may find attending to their listeners' needs relatively easy. They know their people. They visit them, grieve and rejoice with them on a daily basis. Others will have to sense the people's needs through the lens of the world's suffering and spiritual barrenness, and through all those occasions for rejoicing in which communities come together. Sensing need is the beginning of the preaching dialogue. We spend time with the texts seeking to hear the Word and so make connections with the people through what we hear and read. If we do this continually, we will find it quite easy to write them down. Scripted sermons should not sound as if they have been carefully honed for days beforehand. Sermons do not always benefit from being pre-written and then read out, although a scripted sermon is not thereby a bad sermon. It is simply more difficult for people to take what they need from it.

Writing out sermons is the first step in a learning process. Ideally, the preacher should move on from this stage as soon as possible. The longer she relies on her script, the harder it will be to part with it, unless she loses it, as I found when mine fell under my chair. So the next step to be taken on the way to becoming a confident preacher is to *make do with less*. Having written the sermon out in full, and thought deeply about what she has written, the preacher may find that a few bullet points are all she needs. Either way, she must remain open to the possibility of change. Whether or not the preacher chooses to write out a sermon in full, she should always remember that what she thought she wanted to say on Friday afternoon may have changed by Saturday evening. If the sermon is unscripted, notes will help her to stay 'on topic' and limit the risk of omitting crucial points.

Those who like to illustrate their sermon with short relevant anecdotes would be wise to make a note of their next point as, having given the illustration, the nervous preacher risks forgetting what it was she was illustrating, which leaves her flustered and her listeners confused. If you are going to tell a story, make sure your bullet points, or brief notes, remind you of why you are telling it! Similarly, if you are going to refer to names, dates or any other specific facts, it is wise to write them down, even if you are preaching without notes.

This leads to the final and most important element of sermon preparation. Whether or not you choose to write or make notes, *know what you really want to say*. Knowing what you really want to say is not the same as knowing how you are going to say it. For those who prefer not to write the sermon out in full, the latter can obstruct the former. It can also constrain the message, by reducing it to what we think we *ought* to say, or what sounds better. We know what we really want to say because we will have spent much time sensing what God wants to say to his people, sensing the Word. The preacher must not get in the way of the work by obstructing the Word. If possible, he should be able to summarise what he wants to say in a single word because that is the Word on which he is waiting.

As preachers, we live in a state of openness to God for whom we must be prepared to take risks. Perhaps it is this openness which lends itself to what is often mistaken for 'extempore' preaching. The word 'extempore' is defined as 'spoken or done without any preparation or thought'.[5] Such a definition bears no relation to the art of preaching. The sermon must always be prepared and delivered in a considered way, as this book has attempted to illustrate. But the preparing is done to the extent that the preacher's entire life is lived before God, in a state of 'beholding' and of deep inner listening. The commission to 'go and make disciples of all nations' demands nothing less of us. We cannot speak truthfully about God to his people if we ourselves are only partially alive.

When we preach from what we have learned by being present to God at all times and in all places, we bring his life to his people. This is why the prophet Isaiah was so in awe of his task. 'I am a man of unclean lips' he protests (Isaiah 6:5). He did not mean that he was in some way tainted, which is what so much misogynistic and homophobic thinking

---

5   *Cambridge Dictionary.*

derives from. He meant that he feared he was in no way up to the task, any more than the people were fitted to hear God speaking through him. This is a healthy fear and one which we all have to face as preachers. We are indeed not up to the task, but we are in the hands of a faithful God who loves his people and who will give us the gift of speech if only we will ask for it. The coal which touched the prophet's lips was the living fire of the Holy Spirit, promised to us as disciples who are commissioned by Christ with the preaching task (Matt. 28:20).

Finding our voice

It follows that we need to be heard and, phonetically speaking, understood. We are challenged in this area on a number of fronts. We may not have a natural aptitude for voice projection. We may dislike having contraptions such as microphone controls, which need to be switched on and off, in our pockets. We may have a slight, or even severe, speech impediment. None of these things need get in the way of the task in hand provided they are owned and then addressed in practical ways.

Irrespective of the size of the church, or of the distribution of the congregation, we need to know how to make ourselves heard and understood without the help of a microphone. This is a matter of breath control. When we are nervous, which we almost certainly will be, we forget to breathe properly. When this happens, the sound we make has no 'springboard' from which to project and make itself heard by the people at the back. The solution is not to shout. Shouting can come across as aggressive. It can also lead to coughing and, for women, end in a shrill squeak as the throat muscles tighten and block off what little air they have left. Nervous men tend to disappear into themselves and mumble.

If you know someone involved in drama training ask them to show you how to breathe correctly. Otherwise, a basic guideline is to consciously take in the air you need from your diaphragm, the cavity created by your rib cage. The air taken in at this level creates a kind of platform or launching pad for your words. Allow the air you exhale as you speak to project what you are saying, while speaking in a perfectly normal but audible voice. Again, there is no need to shout. Breathing in this way also steadies us and prevents our nervousness taking over. We need a certain amount of nervousness, or what in French is known as 'le trac', in order to perform at all, and preachers are performers in the best sense of the word.

Getting the message across – the 'performance'

Before books were widely available, when the majority of ordinary people could not read, liturgy was drama. It took people out of themselves and brought them into the presence of God. It still does. Good liturgy suspends disbelief. Those who preach play an important part in the drama of liturgy. They are performers who must not obstruct the on-going drama with their personality or appearance, or even by the way they move to the lectern or pulpit. Their leadership style must not obstruct the Word. But preachers do need to be confident and self-aware. They need to be aware of what they sound and look like. They also need to be confident doing what they are doing at any given moment. They must know where things are, including the Bible or text they will be reading from, and the space they will be occupying before, during and after the sermon. They must also know what is required of them in terms of the 'staging' of the service. Not knowing where you are supposed to be at any given moment can be a major distraction and source of anxiety when it comes to preaching. Ask for stage directions before the service if you are unsure of where you should be at any given moment and, in the early days of preaching or taking services, know who to make eye contact with if you think you might forget, or else write yourself some clear instructions. If you have to climb up to a pulpit, check the steps first.

The sermon itself is an integral part of the liturgical drama. Not only is it the bridge between word and sacrament, it brings the people to God. It is the *via sacramenta*, the path and the destination. It is the sacramental Word. The preacher should be mindful of this before she begins to preach. Prefacing the sermon with a short prayer places the people and whatever she will say before God. It also helps to focus attention away from her. The sermon is part of the drama, but the drama is not the preacher performing in his or her own capacity. It is not about us. In being sacrament, it effaces us, and even itself,[6] because it arises from deep silence, a silence held in God.

Maggie Ross writes that *'We need to relearn ancient Christian ways of reading and listening ... We need to learn how to speak slowly, clearly and meaningfully without being artificial so that the living Word*

---

6   'Every true sign effaces itself', Maggie Ross, *Writing the Icon of the Heart*, p.61.

pours through a reader's [or a preacher's] beholding, an emptiness, a receptivity, so that the Word speaks to as many listeners as possible'.[7] The Word speaks into the hearts of the listeners in the way God is to each person; 'I will be what I will be' (Exodus 3:14)[8]. The preaching task is therefore ultimately indefinable, because it is sourced from within the indefinable being of God in which preacher and listeners share. But it is also a living sign of God's on-going activity in the wider world, in the inner being of all people of faith, and even in that of the most convinced atheist. The preached word is part of the unknowing which pertains to the essence of our humanity, to the rational, to the imagination, to memory and to the hopes and fears we carry for the future. The sermon points to the 'waiting' for the completion of God's purpose in Christ's coming again in glory, as he promised.

Ascension Day 2016

---

7   *Ibid.*, p.60.
8   Also translated as 'I am who I am'.

Bibliography

Barker, Margaret, *Temple Theology: An Introduction*, London, SPCK, 2004

Belcher, Jim, *Deep Church: A Third Way Beyond Emerging and Traditional*, Downer's Grove, Illinois, IVP, 2009

Billings, Alan, *Secular Lives, Sacred Hearts: The Role of the Church in a Time of No Religion*, London, SPCK, 2004

Bowen, Roger (ed.), *A Guide to Preaching*, London, SPCK, 2005

Bruce, Kate, *Igniting the Heart: Preaching and Imagination*, London, SCM Press, 2015

Caputo, John D., *Truth: Philosophy in Transit*, London, Penguin, 2013

Carroll, Lewis, *Alice Through the Looking Glass*, London, 1871

Carter Florence, Anna, *Preaching as Testimony*, London, John Knox Press, 2007

Castle, Brian, *Reconciliation: The Journey of a Lifetime*, London, SPCK, 2014

Cavanagh, Lorraine, *Making Sense of God's Love: Atonement and Redemption*, London, SPCK, 2011

Cavanagh, Lorraine, *Finding God in Other Christians*, London, SPCK, 2012

Coggan, Donald, *Preaching: The Sacrament of the Word*, New York, The Crossroad Publishing Company, 1988

Countryman, L. William, *Living on the Border of the Holy: Renewing the Priesthood of All*, Harrisburg, Morehouse Publishing, 1999

– *Calling on the Spirit in Unsettling Times: Discerning God's future for the Church*, Norwich, Canterbury Press, 2012

Cowley, Ian, *The Contemplative Minister: Learning to Lead from the Still Centre*, Oxford, The Bible Reading Fellowship, 2015

Davies, Brian, *An Introduction to the Philosophy of Religion*, Oxford, OUP, 1993

Dearborn, Kerry, *Drinking from the Wells of New Creation: The Holy Spirit and the Imagination in Reconciliation*, Cambridge, James Clarke & Co., 2014

Drane, John, *Do Christians Know How to be Spiritual?: The Rise of New Spirituality and the Mission of the Church*, London, DLT, 2005

Erdozain, Dominic, *The Soul of Doubt: The Religious Roots of Unbelief from Luther to Marx*, Oxford, OUP, 2016

Ford, Michael, *Wounded Prophet: A Portrait of Henri J.M. Nouwen*, London, DLT, 1999

Francis, Leslie J., *Gone But not Forgotten: Church Leaving and Returning*, London, DLT, 1998

Furlong, Monica, *Contemplating Now*, Boston, Cowley Publications, 1971

Hardy, Daniel W., *God's Ways with the World: Thinking and Practising Christian Faith*, Edinburgh, T&T Clark (1996)

   – (with Deborah Hardy Ford, Peter Ochs and David F. Ford) *Wording a Radiance: Parting Conversations on God and the Church*, London, SCM Press, 2010

Haydon Mitchell, Roger, *The Fall of the Church*, Eugene, Oregon, Wipf & Stock, 2013

Jenkins, David E., *God, Jesus and Life in the Spirit*, London, SCM Press, 1988

Joyce, James, *Stephen Hero*, New York, New Directions Publishing Corp, 1944

Lundin, Roger, *Believing Again: Doubt and Faith in a Secular Age*, Grand Rapids, Eerdmans, 2009

McGilchrist, Ian, *The Master and His Emissary: The Divided Brain and the Making of the Western World*, New Haven, Yale University Press, 2012

Newbigin, Lesslie, *The Gospel in a Pluralist Society*, London, SPCK, 1989

Northcutt, Kay L., *Kindling Desire for God: Preaching as Spiritual Direction*, Minneapolis, Fortress Press, 2009

Nouwen, Henri J.M., *With Burning Hearts: A Meditation on the Eucharistic Life*, Maryknoll, New York, Orbis Books, 1994

Ross, Maggie, *Silence: A User's Guide*, London, DLT, 2014

– *Pillars of Flame: Power, Priesthood and Spiritual Maturity*, New York, Seabury Books, 2007

– *Writing the Icon of the Heart: In Silence Beholding*, Abingdon, Bible Reading Fellowship, 2011

Tillich, Paul, *Systematic Theology*, Chicago, University of Chicago Press, 1951

Tomlinson, Dave, *Re-Enchanting Christianity*, Norwich, Canterbury Press, 2008

Volf, Miroslav, *Exclusion and Embrace: A Theological Exploration of Identity, Otherness and Reconciliation*, Nashville, Abingdon Press, 1996

Wallace, James A., *Preaching to the Hungers of the Heart: The Homily on the Feasts and with the Rites*, Collegeville, Minnesota, Liturgical Press, 2002

Weil, Simone, *Waiting on God* (Emma Craufurd tr.), Glasgow, Collins Fount, 1951

Whitehead, James D. and Whitehead, Evelyn Eaton, *Nourishing the Spirit: The Healing Emotions of Wonder, Joy, Compassion, and Hope*, Maryknoll, Orbis, 2012